SAFE

Suzanne P. Starseed

Printed in the U.S.A.
ISBN: 978-0-578-64504-9

In-Sync Therapy, Inc.
9702 Gayton Road
Suite 323
Richmond, VA
23238

www.suzannestarseed.com

For my parents,
who encouraged me to think for myself
and always loved me.

CONTENTS

Have we fallen into a mesmerized state that makes us accept as inevitable that which is inferior or detrimental, as though having lost the will or the vision to demand that which is good?

Rachel Carson, *Silent Spring.*

Letter to the Reader

I finished the manuscript for this book in mid-February during the quiet before the full force of the tsunami of COVID-19 reached our shores. As I write this, I am at home in Richmond, Virginia. Our schools closed two weeks ago and yesterday our governor issued a stay-at-home order. Uncertainty prevails. Our lives are disrupted in ways we could not have imagined a few weeks ago. And people are dying. Uncertainty fuels our fears.

My fear is that the vulnerabilities and inequalities that I discuss in my book will lead to unnecessary devastation. That having worshipped the false god of competition at the expense of cooperation and compassion for so long, we have lost our moral compass and veered so far off course into income inequality and disregard for Life and quality of life that this tsunami will leave a traumatized nation in its wake.

One of the things researchers have discovered about trauma is that we retain a sense of being threatened long after the threat is gone. In SAFE, I discuss the research on trauma's potential, long-term negative impact on our relationships, ability to regulate our emotions, and our ability to think clearly and solve problems. The research also shows that the single most important factor in resilience to and recovery from trauma is social connectedness and emotional support.

SAFE

I think Mr. Rogers has given us the best advice for coping with the stress and social distancing we are experiencing in these uncertain times: "In times of stress, the best thing we can do for each other is to listen with our ears and our hearts and to be assured that our questions are just as important as our answers." It is my hope that when the immediate threat of the virus has subsided, we can listen to each other, support each other, and come together to build a more secure nation.

Suzanne P. Starseed

Chapter 1

Attunement

Brains need caring more than caring needs brains.
                                                    -Sarah Blaffer Hrdy

In 2018, the Virginia State Legislature passed a bill barring schools from suspending students in preschool through third grade for more than three days. Virginia isn't alone; other states including Maryland, Ohio, Colorado, and Texas have passed or considered such a ban, particularly for preschools. Why would our elected officials think such a remedy was necessary? At an alarming rate, schools throughout the U.S. have been using what are called exclusionary discipline practices, suspension and expulsion, in response to the "challenging" behavior of young children.

During the 2016-17 school year, Virginia public schools issued nearly 18,000 short-term suspensions and at least 111 long-term suspensions just to children in preschool through 3rd grade. The 2016 National Survey of Children's Health, found that an estimated 50,000 *preschoolers* were suspended at least once that year. Another 17,000 preschoolers are estimated to have been expelled.

What are these challenging behaviors that are getting three to five-year- olds disciplined so harshly? The most common reasons are prolonged tantrums, noncompliance, disruptive behavior, property destruction, physical and verbal aggression, and withdrawal. In short, behaviors that young children who have poorly developed emotional and behavioral self-regulation show when they are under stress. Traditional punishment and reward disciplinary practices are ineffective with highly stressed children, so their teachers are at a loss for how to manage their difficult behaviors.

This situation begs two questions: Why are preschoolers experiencing so much stress? And why are some of them not developing the age-appropriate self-regulation of their emotions and behavior needed to cope with the inevitable stress and challenges of daily life? The answer to both of these questions can be found in our fast-paced technological culture, economic realities, and educational policy. As a society, our basic assumptions about what our children need to grow and thrive and our expectations for their behavior have diverged from children's natural developmental needs and normal developmental trajectories.

The development of self-regulation is very similar to the development of speech. Babies are born with the potential to develop both of these, but it takes consistent, predictable interactions with caregivers in the context of safe secure relationships for normal development to unfold. When babies are uncomfortable; when they are hungry, wet, in pain, or physically uncomfortable in some other way, they are completely dependent on adults to meet their physical needs and sooth their emotions. Physically and emotionally responsive adult care is a basic survival need. As caregivers consistently help babies and young children move from a distressed state to feeling calm, comfortable and safe, young children gradually learn how to do this for themselves, to self-regulate.

Another important foundation of self-regulation is the secure parent-child relationship that comes from what the Center on the Developing Child at Harvard University calls "serve and return" interaction. In safe and supportive circumstances, parents and their children dance together in an attuned call and response in which the baby or toddler reaches out for interaction through babbling, facial expressions, gestures, and words, and the parent responds in kind. This "serve and return" interaction supports optimal brain development. If a caregivers' responses are unreliable, inappropriate, or simply absent, it interferes with the development of a secure parent-child relationship and self-regulation.

Some developmental psychologists have become concerned that parents' habitual smart phone use may disrupt the attuned dance of emotional connection and have a negative effect on their children's social-emotional development. "Technoference" is what researchers call the psychological withdrawal and non-responsiveness that comes with smart phone use. A number of studies have found that parents' habitual mobile-device use can interfere with their child's development of self-regulation.

Because children are so utterly dependent on caregivers to meet their physical and emotional needs, babies come hardwired to interpret emotionally unresponsive care as a threat to their survival. In the absence of emotional responsiveness, their brains automatically activate a physiological fight-flight-freeze stress response to the threat. Videos made by child development researchers show how truly instinctive the need for emotional responsiveness is. In these videos, mothers and their babies are happily engaged in the attuned dance of coos and facial expressions until the mother switches to an entirely blank facial expression. As soon as she switches to what researchers call a "still" face, her baby becomes distressed and may start crying.

What happens to children who don't receive consistent emotionally responsive attuned caregiving? This ongoing threat to their survival causes a repeated triggering of the fight-flight-freeze stress response, flooding their brains and bodies with stress hormones. Scientists call this chronic triggering of the stress response "toxic stress" and tell us it interferes with a child's overall brain development and specifically with the development of self-regulation.

Dr. John Bowlby, the pioneering British psychiatrist who studied the effect of separation from parents and emotionally unresponsive caregiving in orphanages, had already documented the devastation wrought on children by the absence of consistent emotionally responsive caregiving. But these lessons were not in the American consciousness until hundreds of couples brought their adopted children home from Eastern European orphanages following the breakup of the Soviet Union. These children had been physically cared for but their emotional needs were not met. The most egregious emotional neglect occurred in Romanian orphanages.

The children these loving couples brought home from Romania characteristically responded to the most benign circumstances with a fight-flight-freeze response as if they were under threat or they withdrew and shut down. Their poor self-regulation and aggressive behavior got them into trouble and alienated them from their adoptive families who found traditional disciplinary methods didn't work.

In my clinical practice, I worked with a family who had adopted a 13-year-old boy "second hand" from an East European orphanage. His first set of adoptive parents had thrown in the towel and this couple responded to a plea from their church to take him in. I understand why his first set of adoptive parents had given up on him; he was in fight-or-flight, like a caged animal, most of the time. In fact, his new parents found it necessary to create a cage for him in the back seat of their car by putting a barrier between the front and back seats to prevent him from attacking the driver.

Brain imaging studies of children who have experienced severe emotional neglect show smaller brains and a lower quality electrical brain activity as measured by EEG. These children exhibit poor impulse control, social withdrawal, low self-esteem, pathological behaviors such as tics, tantrums, stealing, and self-punishment – in short, poor self-regulation. They also have poor intellectual functioning and low academic achievement. Some of these brain changes and associated behavior can potentially be reversed. The younger a child is adopted into a loving family, the better the prognosis.

Scientists have found that repeated experiences can change our brains, both positively and negatively, through two primary mechanisms. These are called neural plasticity and epigenetic modification. Through neural plasticity, our repeated experiences literally rewire our brains. Neural connections that are used repeatedly become stronger and become our brains' default settings for thought, behavior, and emotion. Connections rarely used are deleted or "pruned". Brain changes produced through neural plasticity occur throughout our lives, but the younger we are the more plastic our brains. This is why the outcomes for the Romanian orphans were better the younger they were adopted.

Most of us were taught that the genes we inherited from our parents are unchangeable blueprints for our bodies, our health, and our intelligence. But scientists have discovered that's not the whole picture. Although we come into the world with a particular set of genes, these genes can be turned on and off or "expressed" as a result of our repeated interactions with the physical and social environment through a mechanism called epigenetic modification. This is one of the ways nurturing changes brain development.

The Romanian orphans are an extreme and tragic example of what happens when children don't receive the emotional nurturing they need. But neural plasticity is continuously shaping our brains in response to *repeated **positive** experiences* as well as negative. Some of the Romanian children who were moved to foster care or adopted by their second birthday had essentially normal EEG activity by the time they were eight. Other studies of U.S. foster children, who had abnormal stress hormone patterns, showed a return to normal stress hormone patterns when they were given attuned emotionally responsive foster parenting. However, foster children given more traditional punishment and reward parenting did not show improved stress hormone patterns and associated behavioral changes.

Other, less dramatically stressful life circumstances can produce lesser degrees of the same sorts of brain and behavior changes seen in the orphans. A substantial body of scientific evidence shows that growing up in poverty or other very stressful family and community circumstances such as domestic or community violence can negatively impact brain development too. The areas of the brain most affected by stress are those responsible for self-regulation, social connection, and executive functions like attention, problem solving, and empathy. Deficits in these functions can create social, emotional, and behavioral challenges for children that lead to diagnoses that range from Attention Deficit Disorder to Generalized Anxiety Disorder to Oppositional Defiant Disorder.

Clearly high levels of stress are not good for children. They aren't good for adults either. Although the stress most of us experience day to day doesn't meet the threshold of toxic stress, its effects seem pretty toxic to me. We are living in an age of anxiety and stress is so pervasive in our lives that we have come to accept it as normal. Some of us have our internal thermostats set point for "normal" at such a high level of stress that calm feels alien and a bit boring. We require a stressful level of stimulation to keep us going.

So, what is stress – really? We use the word with many different meanings for different circumstances. We say "I was stressed out all day." or "She stressed how important this is to her." or "His cardiologist ordered a stress test". Scientifically speaking, a stressor is anything outside of us that disrupts or threatens our internal physiological or psychological homeostatic balance. A stress response is what we do to regain the safety of homeostasis.

What is this homeostasis we are seeking? Homeostasis comes from *homeo* meaning "similar to" or "resembling" and *stasis* meaning a stable state. So regaining homeostasis is an attempt to return to a safe stable state that is very like the state we were in before the disruption, to our personal "normal". The classic example of homeostasis is maintaining a steady body temperature by sweating when we are hot and shivering when we are cold. Homeostasis is the normal "set point" of our internal thermostat. When we are pushed from or lose our homeostatic balance, a response is triggered to return us to the safety of our normal. This is often true even when we are pushed toward something better.

Homeostasis is not just an individual sport; it's a team sport too. Members of a social group can cooperate to maintain a safe stable state in response to a disruption or threat to the group. We see this when a colony of bees cooperate to promote the health of the colony by fanning their wings to cool the hive. Homeostasis is a survival response whether individual or group.

Parenthood or impending parenthood can add an additional layer of stress to people's lives whether the pregnancy was intended or not. When we adopted our much-hoped-for daughter, it was like dropping a bomb into our lives. Everything changed and change is stressful. We are all hard-wired to need a certain amount of predictability and control to feel safe. Uncertainty is stressful and we will seek certainty and strive for control at almost any cost.

Our attempts to gain the security of control and predictability can be maladaptive and ripple out, affecting those around us. Stress diminishes our emotional self-regulation and our ability to focus, think rationally, and solve problems. To top it off, scientists tell us stress is contagious due to our "mirror" neural networks - we unconsciously and automatically imitate the emotions and states of others in the same way we automatically smile back when a stranger smiles at us.

As humans we have the unique ability to turn on a stress response by thinking about future *potential* stressors that may throw us out of our "normal" - or hoped for - homeostatic balance. We not only mount a physiological fight-flight-freeze stress response to physical or psychological insults; we can mount one in the expectation of disruption. Psychologists call this anxiety.

Most scientific discussions of stress are based on animal studies and emphasize physiological and behavioral fight-flight-freeze responses. As social beings, we are wired to seek the safety of others before we trigger a full-blown physiological stress response. Reaching out for connection to others is baked into our survival instincts from the beginning and this does not go away. Social connection reduces our stress. In 1958 Dr. John Bowlby, the father of Attachment Theory, wrote in a letter to his wife: "Most people think of fear as running away from something. But there is another side to it. We run TO someone, usually a person .... It's screamingly obvious, but I believe it to be a new idea, and quite revolutionary"

Just as children need emotional connection to their mothers and other caregivers to thrive, so mothers need supportive emotional connections with those around them so they have the inner resources to provide attuned, emotionally responsive care to their children. Parenthood makes people feel less safe, especially mothers. Suddenly, parents are vulnerable in a way they could not have anticipated. As some wise person is oft quoted as saying, "When you are a mother, you wear your heart outside your body." This is an incredibly vulnerable state to be in.

When mothers are stressed, their ability to be emotionally responsive to their infants is compromised. Our society pays lip service to the value of motherhood, but our modern society fails to deliver the emotional and material support mothers and their children need to feel safe and to thrive.

I consider myself a feminist and have been one of the many beneficiaries of the women's movement, having had a successful and fulfilling career. I'm grateful to have been in an economic and career position to be able to work part-time after adopting our daughter so I could give her the emotionally responsive care she needed. In today's economy, many women don't have that luxury.

In the U.S., seventy percent of mothers with children under 18 participate in the labor force, with over seventy-five percent of those employed full-time. Mothers are the primary or sole earners for forty percent of households with children under 18 today, compared with eleven percent in 1960. In almost half of households with a mother and father, both parents are employed full time.

Three in ten U.S. mothers return to work within two months of their babies' birth. Mothers who are young and have low incomes, and those with lower levels of education often return to work even earlier. The main reason so many mothers' return to work so soon after giving birth is that the U.S. does not mandate *any* paid maternity leave. We are the only developed country in the world that fails to support the health and well-being of mothers and babies by mandating paid family leave. This, in spite of the fact, that paid leave is associated with reduced infant mortality and improved child and maternal health. The first few months following birth are critical for the family to settle in and provide the consistent responsive loving care that builds secure attachment.

The U.S. also falls short on availability of affordable high-quality child care. Parents looking for child care, sometimes desperately, have little freedom of choice.

There are three main types of child care available to families. One is "family care" that can be in a licensed family child care home or unlicensed family, friend, or neighbor care. Another type is child care centers which are generally operated out of non-residential, commercial buildings and group children by age. These centers are larger, enroll more children, and have a dedicated director and numerous staff members. The third type, preschool programs for children ages 3-5 years old, are typically offered through a school, faith-based organization, non-profit organization, or a child care center.

Cost and quality can vary widely within each type of child care. In the U.S., the average cost of childcare is between $9,000 and $9,600 per year per child. This makes us one of the least affordable developed nations for child care, as measured by percentage of family income. The cost standard set for affordable child care by the U.S. Department of Health and Human Services is no more than 7% of a family's income. Seventy-one percent of families spend 10% or more of their annual income on child care. A third of those families spend 20% and nearly one-fifth of the families spend a whopping 25% of their income on child care.

Regardless of quality, the cost of child care is beyond the reach of many parents. They are caught between caring for their children and the need to provide for them. Other parents balance precariously with fragile, piece meal child care that can fall apart at any time causing them to miss work. Even parents with solid child care arrangements are vulnerable to missing work and potential job loss if their child has physical or mental health issues. In 2016 alone, the National Survey of Children's Health found that an estimated two million parents of children aged five and younger had to quit a job, not take a job, or significantly change their job because of problems with child care.

According to Harvard's Center on the Developing Child, the six primary characteristics of high-quality child care are a safe physical setting, small group sizes, a language-rich environment, developmentally appropriate activities, high adult-child ratios, and *warm and responsive adult-child interactions.*

Research on the effectiveness of early childhood programs focuses largely on short-term academic gains in child care centers. While center-based care can raise reading and math scores, research evidence suggests it can have a negative effect on social behavior. Studies have found that extensive daycare experience is associated with poor emotional self-regulation, rule-breaking, irritability, belligerence, and negative interactions. The part of the brain responsible for self-regulation goes through the most rapid growth during the preschool years making it most powerfully shaped by repeated experiences of self-regulation or dysregulation before entering first grade.

Stress is the primary contributing factor to the dysregulated behavior reported in these studies. Research on the stress hormone cortisol found that many children attending daycare showed atypical cortisol patterns similar to those seen in U.S. children in foster care and in children from Romanian orphanages. This contrasts with the healthy cortisol pattern seen in children not attending daycare. These results aren't limited to low-quality child care. High-quality child care centers that offered pre-kindergarten academics and "sensitive responsive" teachers were also linked to atypical cortisol patterns. This research brings up the question of whether the stress associated with daycare is contributing to the current epidemic of attention deficit disorder.

If children are experiencing high levels of stress in child care, what's causing it? Scientists have identified two potential factors, not mutually exclusive. One is the stress of not having a consistently attuned, emotionally responsive caregiver during the day, and the second is the stress of extended interaction with peers. Researchers found that children with more secure attachments to teachers were less likely to show an atypical cortisol pattern. Furthermore, there is evidence that some children may be buffered against developing an atypical cortisol pattern by a secure mother-child attachment. Some research suggests that a secure attachment with a caregiver in daycare may compensate for the adverse effects of an insecure parent-child relationship at home.

The second factor is the stress of extended interaction with peers. There's less research to support this hypothesis but I know from my own experience as a mother that young children are, well, immature and there's bound to be conflict when they spend a lot of time together in a group. Children are more likely to behave better with just one or two friends. By their nature children have difficulty controlling their emotions and aren't known for sensitivity to the needs of others. Interaction with older children and adults is more predictable and less stressful for young children.

In addition to the potential stressors identified by researchers, I've identified a third stressor which is increasingly present in child care today. It is the indirect result of national educational legislation passed in 2001 and repealed in 2015 that required high- stakes standardized testing in reading and math starting in the third grade. The legacy of this No Child Left Behind legislation, passed in 2001, is that reading instruction has been pushed down into kindergarten and preschool before most children are developmentally ready to learn to read. This mismatch between what young children are developmentally equipped to do and the academic demands placed on them causes enormous stress and too often a sense of shame or feeling stupid. This is especially true for children in vulnerable populations such as those living in poverty.

To look at the long-term impact of academic instruction compared with more traditional nursery school activities, one study compared the effects of three different preschool curriculum models on academic and social outcomes of children born in poverty, following them until they were 23 years old. In the Direct Instruction model, teachers directly taught children academic skills, rewarding them for correct answers to the teacher's questions. In the second model, called the Nursery School model, teachers responded to children's self-initiated play in a loosely structured, socially supportive setting. And in the third model, the High/Scope Preschool Curriculum (Perry Preschool Project), teachers set up the classroom and the daily routine so that children could plan, do, and review their own activities and engage in active developmentally appropriate learning experiences individually, in small groups, and in whole-class groups.

The Direct Instruction model showed temporary gains in academic performance but in the long-term the children had more emotional problems and *felony arrests*. At age 15 the Direct Instruction group reported committing 2½ times as many acts of misconduct as the High/Scope group. At age 23, compared to the other curriculum groups, the Direct Instruction group had three times as many felony arrests per person, especially those involving property crimes. Incredibly, 47% of the Direct Instruction group was treated for emotional impairment or disturbance during their schooling, as compared to only 6% of either of the other curriculum groups. The researchers conclude that "these findings argue against using Direct Instruction in preschool programs and for using a well-defined curriculum model based on child-initiated learning activities."

The shift to early academics in our country has decreased the time teachers can spend on more developmentally appropriate activities and on building trusting, emotionally responsive relationships with their students. The effects of this shift and evidence-based educational alternatives to it are covered in much greater depth in my book *The Ecology of Learning: Re-Inventing Schools.*

As a nation, we could fairly easily remedy this source of our children's stress and emotional dysregulation by returning preschools and kindergartens to the kinder and gentler environments they were before No Child Left Behind. We can do this without setting our children's academic achievement back because teaching children to read earlier does not make them better readers in the long term. Most European countries, with better educational outcomes than ours, delay direct reading instruction until age seven when their students are developmentally ready and can learn to read more quickly, easily, and with less sense of failure. This approach gives teachers the time they need to support children's development in more appropriate ways, leading to better, long-term outcomes.

As a nation, we have failed to adapt to the majority of women entering the workforce in ways that meet the physical, emotional, and learning needs of our children. Our policies related to family leave, childcare, and education have left parents and children stressed and less able to cope with change and the challenges of daily life. It's time for us to acknowledge this and work together to develop policies that promote the well-being of parents and children and thus create a better future for us all.

Chapter 2

Adversity

In the little world in which children have their existence, whosoever brings them up, there is nothing so finely perceived and so finely felt, as injustice.

-Charles Dickens

In 2019 on a weekend in early August two mass shootings in less than 24 hours left at least 31 people dead and 50 injured. The shootings took place 1,600 miles apart in Dayton, Ohio and El Paso, Texas. As I write this one week later, a mixture of fear, anger, and compassion for the victims radiates out across our nation and saturates our news cycle. We ask ourselves; how can this keep happening and what could we have done to prevent it? Instead of answers, we get recriminations and blame from the politicians and pundits.

It's time to look more deeply at the question of why some people are capable of such hatred and violence toward complete strangers. What are the conditions that give rise to such violence? A partial answer lies in childhood adversity. A study funded by the U.S. Justice Department that drilled down into every shooting incident at schools, workplaces, and places of worship since 1999 found the vast majority of mass shooters experienced early childhood trauma and exposure to violence at a young age. The nature of their exposure included parental suicide; emotional, physical or sexual abuse; neglect; domestic violence; and/or severe bullying. This trauma was often a precursor to mental health problems, including depression, anxiety, thought disorders, or suicidality.

How we treat children matters. The adversity these shooters experienced as children is not as uncommon as we would like to think and the negative consequences of childhood adversity pervade our society. A substantial body of research shows a strong correlation between how children are treated, their emotions, and their physical and mental health as adults. The Adverse Childhood Experiences (ACE) study that first ignited the burst of scientific inquiry into the effects of childhood adversity was conducted by Dr. Vincent Felitti of the Kaiser Permanente Department of Preventive Medicine and Robert Anda from the Centers for Disease Control and Prevention between 1995 and 1997.

The study involved giving medical screenings to and taking social and medical histories from over 17,000 middle to upper-middle class, racially diverse, mostly college educated adults. Participants were also asked to complete a questionnaire about their childhood experiences. The questionnaire asked only 10 "yes" or "no" questions about physical, emotional and sexual abuse; physical and emotional neglect; living with a family member who was addicted to alcohol or other substances, or who was depressed or had other mental illnesses; experiencing parental divorce or separation; having a family member who was incarcerated; and witnessing a mother being abused. (See in Appendix A for the full questionnaire.) Each participant was given an ACE score from 1 to 10 based on their number of "yes" responses.

Once the numbers had been crunched and the data analyzed, the pattern that emerged was astounding. In this middle-class educated group of people, one in nine had an ACE score of 5 or more. Childhood emotional and physical neglect, abuse, and the toxic stress of emotional disconnection from parents was much more prevalent than anyone had imagined. It had been off our society's radar, hidden in secrecy and shame.

More discomforting was the impact these adverse childhood experiences had on the trajectories of their adult lives. As the ACE score increases, so does the risk of disease and social and emotional problems. With an ACE score of 4 or more, things start getting serious. Having an ACE score of 4 nearly doubles the risk of heart disease and cancer and it increases the risk of chronic pulmonary lung disease by nearly 400 percent. An ACE score of 4 or more increases the likelihood of becoming a self-acknowledged alcoholic by 700 percent, of depression 460 percent, and the risk of attempted suicide increases by 1200 percent. People with an ACE score of 6 or higher are at risk of their lifespan being shortened by 20 years. ACEs are responsible for a large proportion of workplace absenteeism and for health care, emergency response, mental health, and criminal justice costs.

Dr. Felitti and his colleagues concluded that "Adverse childhood experiences are the most basic causes of health risk behaviors, morbidity, disability, mortality, and health care costs" in the U.S. Subsequent studies have shown an even higher prevalence of childhood adversity in other more vulnerable populations. These studies found that growing up with poverty, homelessness, community violence, and/or racial discrimination are associated with significant negative mental and physical health consequences in adulthood. Children with ADHD have a higher incidence of exposure to ACEs and justice-involved youth are four times more likely to report 4 or more ACEs than the adults in the original ACE study. More than three in four (76.3 percent) U.S. children ages 3-5 who were expelled from preschool had ACEs.

When most of us think of trauma, what usually comes to mind is a single horrible event either from our own experience or from media images of disasters or violence. But the hidden childhood trauma documented in the ACE study is different: No one was watching and documenting the trauma, and no one came to the rescue. The trauma was embedded in the children's daily lives and normalized - a "death by a thousand cuts."

It is repeated experiences, researchers tell us, that are most likely to result in altered brain architecture and function, especially in developing brains. In the case of most adverse childhood experiences, the parents are frequently unavailable, unaware, rejecting, or even dangerous. This consistent sense of emotional disconnection or fear creates chronic toxic stress and shame.

The physiological and behavioral effects of chronic toxic stress are the mechanisms by which adverse childhood experiences translate into negative physical and mental health outcomes for adults. Through neural plasticity, the repeated experiences of threat and the triggering of the fight- flight-freeze response, with its flood of stress hormones, strengthens the stress-associated neural connections and prunes less used neural connections. Thus, the fight-flight-freeze response becomes the brain's immediate unconscious default setting both physiologically and behaviorally. This has profound physical and emotional consequences, as international trauma specialist Dr. Bessel van der Kolk tells us in his book, *The Body Keeps the Score*.

Chronic stress with its repeated triggering of the fight- flight-freeze response impairs children's self- regulation, their ability to learn, and their interpretation of social cues. Stress is what scientists call a "motivational state", like hunger. The state of toxic stress causes us to interpret our experiences and the intentions of others through the lens of fear. Responding in a fearful way, stressed children often over-react and get in trouble. Their challenging behavior elicits punishment and pushes adults away from them just when they need the safety of an adult connection the most. Positive emotional connection calms the fight- flight-freeze response.

There is a second mechanism that Dr. Felitti and subsequent researchers have identified as contributing to the negative health and behavioral consequences of childhood trauma - self-medicating emotional pain. Dr. Felitti concluded, "The ACE Study provides population-based clinical evidence that unrecognized adverse childhood experiences are a major, if not the major, determinant of who turns to psychoactive materials and becomes addicted." Adult addiction is deeply tied to childhood trauma, in part, because it makes adults more vulnerable to stress.

Adverse childhood experiences make adults less resilient and able to cope with adversity. The research shows that the likelihood of turning to drugs, alcohol, or nicotine as a coping strategy to deal with stress, anxiety, and emotional pain increases proportionally to the intensity of adverse childhood experiences in a strong, graded, dose-response manner. At the extreme end of this stepwise progression, a male child with an ACE Score of 6 has a 4,600% increase in the likelihood of becoming an injection drug user when compared to a male child with an ACE Score of 0. A similar graded dose-response pattern holds for nicotine and alcohol. Someone with an ACE score of six is 250% more likely to be a smoker than someone with an ACE score of zero. And people with an ACE score of four or more are 700% more likely to self-report alcoholism than someone with zero adverse childhood experiences.

A recent study of patients at a rural opioid use disorder clinic reported that almost half of the patients had ACE scores of four or more. The researchers found that 54% of all patients relapsed back into opioid use after treatment and that the higher the ACE score the more likely a patient will relapse.

Many addiction experts think that addiction is a normal response to the adversity experienced in childhood, just like bleeding is a normal response to being stabbed. Dr. Daniel Sumrok, director of the Center for Addiction Sciences at the University of Tennessee Health Science Center's College of Medicine says addiction shouldn't be called "addiction." Instead, it should be called "ritualized compulsive comfort-seeking."

The implications of these ACE studies are overwhelming. The first time I read about them, I felt so disheartened and helpless I cried. I still get emotional when I think of the maltreatment of so many children by the adults responsible for *caring* for them. Then I have to stop myself and feel compassion for the caregivers as well. Their own childhood adversity and life circumstances may make them less able to cope with the stress of parenting. We are all caught in this crazy dance of survival together.

So, what can we as individuals and as a society do to turn this destructive cycle around? To create a virtuous cycle? We are not helpless but most of us are unaware and so cannot act on our better instincts.

Now that we know how powerful children's emotions and social connections are for good or ill, how do we use this awareness in our own relationships with family and friends? To begin with, we can think twice before criticizing, shaming, or blaming them. And we can stop demeaning our children.

The first question on the ACE study questionnaire is "Did a parent or other adult in the household often or very often… Swear at you, insult you, put you down, or humiliate you?" A "yes" response to this question will give you an ACE score of 1.

Our dependence on emotional connection for survival from birth leads to an instinctive interpretation of criticism and blame as rejection and, therefore, as a threat. As adults, with our fully developed brains and capacity for self-regulation, we can more objectively consider the validity of criticism and blame leveled at us and curb our emotional responses to it. Some of us are better at this than others, perhaps as a result of our childhood experiences.

Children can't make an objective assessment of the validity of criticism. It goes straight into their hearts and makes them feel rejected and unworthy. It creates shame that embeds in their consciousness as a sense of being flawed and unlovable. I think many of us can feel this in ourselves if we give it our full attention. When you are critical of yourself, whose voice do you hear in your head?

The original ACE study questionnaire did not ask specifically about spanking. The closest it came is in the second part of the first question: "or Act in a way that made you afraid that you might be physically hurt?" I think spanking or threatening to spank a child warrants a "yes" to this question no matter how much we have normalized it. Subsequent ACE studies asked about spanking and found that being spanked as a child was significantly associated with negative mental health outcomes. Other studies over the last two decades have thoroughly documented the negative effects of spanking. These include increased child aggression and anxiety, increased risk for emotional disorders such as depression, lower self-esteem, cognitive difficulties, and more negative relationships between children and their parents.

According to the research, spanking is not effective in stopping children from engaging in disruptive behaviors. It may gain short term compliance from a child, but studies show that, in the long term, spanking is associated with *less* compliance than other forms of discipline. In its December 2018 policy statement, "Effective Discipline to Raise Healthy Children", the American Academy of Pediatrics opposed the use of spanking as a disciplinary measure. They said "Research has shown that striking a child, yelling at or shaming them can elevate stress hormones and lead to changes in the brain's architecture. Harsh verbal abuse is also linked to mental health problems in preteens and adolescents."

Instead of spanking, the American Academy of Pediatrics encourages parents to use positive reinforcement as a primary means of teaching acceptable behavior. They recommend using healthy forms of discipline that are less likely to trigger a fight-flight-freeze response, such as limit setting, redirecting, and setting expectations. Proactive measures that build trust and positive parent-child relationships can decrease disruptive behavior and the need for discipline.

When children seriously misbehave, can't focus, or are impulsive, it's usually because they are stressed and feeling threatened.

Disciplinary measures that threaten or further stress the child are counterproductive because of the way our brain's automatic risk assessment system works. All of us, human and animal, have a subconscious system for detecting threats that scans our environment continuously for the level of risk. This scanning process is called "neuroception" a term coined by neuropsychologist Stephen Porges.

Neuroception is why a baby coos at a caregiver but cries at a stranger, or why a toddler enjoys a parent's embrace but views a hug from a stranger as an assault. The process of neuroception automatically and *unconsciously* determines whether situations and people are safe, dangerous, or life threatening. Based on this unconscious assessment, our bodies automatically respond by shifting the balance of our autonomic nervous system to one of three fundamental physiological states.

When our neuroception tells us we are safe, our autonomic nervous system moves into a calm, relaxed state and we are able to activate our social engagement system. This is the system responsible for reading and responding appropriately to social cues. It allows us to engage in attuned reciprocal social interaction through facial expressions, voice quality, and interpretation of speech. In this state we are able to access our higher order thinking, solve problems, and experience positive emotions.

When we subconsciously perceive that we are threatened, before we mount a full fight-flight-freeze response, our first instinct is to turn to social connection; to reach out for help, support, or comfort from the people around us. Positive social connections help calm our nervous system and regulate our emotional state.

When we reach out for connection, if no one comes to our aid or if we're in immediate danger, our autonomic nervous system shifts to the second physiological state, fight-or-flight. In this stress state, we are cut off from our social engagement system, our rational thinking, and capacity for problem solving. We become more impulsive; our attention focuses on the perceived danger; and we are biased to action, to fight or flee to protect ourselves. We are more likely to experience anger and other negative emotions in this state. The third state of freeze or collapse occurs when we feel trapped or helpless to protect ourselves.

Our assessment of the level of risk in a situation is automatic, subconscious, and tied to our previous experiences, especially repeated experiences. Through neural plasticity, we develop default settings for the subconscious interpretation of situations and people as safe or threatening. The Center on the Developing Child at Harvard University tells us that "For young children who perceive the world as a threatening place, a wide range of conditions can trigger anxious behaviors that then impair their ability to learn and to interact socially with others."

The subconscious nature of neuroception can create a disconnect between our physiological state and our conscious assessment of a situation. That's what's happening when we feel like someone is creepy, but there is no objective reason for this judgement. If our neuroception is accurate, it contributes to keeping us emotionally and physically safe.

Adults who have experienced trauma or a high degree of adversity in childhood often have faulty neuroception. They may misinterpret other's actions and intentions as threatening, creating havoc in their relationships with family, friends, and in the work place. Stephen Porges believes faulty neuroception might lie at the root of several psychiatric disorders, including autism, anxiety disorders, depression, Reactive Attachment Disorder, Oppositional Defiant Disorder, and Conduct Disorder. My clinical experience points to the possibility that faulty neuroception is the root of Attention Deficit Disorder too.

When we think of fight-flight-freeze we assume it refers to fear, but fear is an emotional label we put on the sense of threat when we can identify a specific objective cause for it. Neuroscientist Joseph LeDoux cautions us not to call the autonomic physiological fight-flight-freeze stress response a "fear" response because it can be triggered unconsciously by things that, logically, aren't scary. He prefers the term "defensive survival response" and says we intellectually interpret and give different emotional meanings to this stress state. For example, skydivers experience a flood of stress hormones when they jump from a plane and call it an exciting "adrenaline rush". Many would call that same rush of stress hormones "terror". We may interpret the stress we are experiencing as fear, anxiety, irritability, dread, worry, stress, anger, overwhelm, or excitement and thrill depending on the context and our past experiences. We can experience different emotions in the same physiological fight-flight-freeze state.

Scientists tell us that unless we are actually in a dangerous situation, our fight-flight-freeze response does not serve us well. The negative physical consequences of prolonged stress are well documented in the scientific literature. When a fight-flight-freeze response is triggered, our brains automatically initiate a cascade of neurotransmitters and stress hormones that affect almost every system of our bodies. Blood pressure and heart rate go up and immune function is suppressed. Blood sugar levels increase and we are more likely to crave sugary and high-fat foods.

We become more vigilant, on edge, and sensitive to incoming stimuli that can signal danger. Changes occur in our vision, hearing, motor control, attention, memory, and intellectual function. We filter incoming information for its survival value, paying attention to and remembering the things that are potential threats and ignoring other aspects of the situation. Our self-control is diminished; we are more impulsive and less patient. In a fight-flight-freeze state our rational thinking, mental flexibility, and executive function skills are diminished so we are less able to think clearly, solve problems, plan, organize, and be creative.

Fear of failure or shame can trigger the fight-flight-freeze response we call test anxiety. I had such extreme test-anxiety while taking the exam required for admission to graduate school, that I had trouble understanding the *instructions* for the math section. People who have a fear of public speaking experience the effects of fight-flight-freeze on intellectual function and memory when their minds go blank in front of an audience.

When we don't feel safe, uncertainty makes us feel even more threatened. Under stress we are all hardwired to try to protect ourselves through gaining more control and predictability. Feeling unsafe can reduce our flexibility and it can make us seem more "oppositional" and emotionally defensive. In children, this shows up as non-compliance.

At the Ainsworth Attachment Clinic in Charlottesville, Virginia I had the opportunity to discuss non-compliance and oppositional behavior with its director, Robert Marvin, an internationally recognized expert in the field of attachment and trauma. I told him my theory is that when kids are highly stressed, "no" is the safest response (even to things they would ordinarily like) because they can't control or predict what will happen on the other side of "yes". His response was "But they can say 'yes' if there's someone they *trust* on the other side of 'yes'." With a trusted person metaphorically holding the child's hand, the bridge to "yes" can be crossed together.

This is the power of trust and connection. It helps us feel safe and it alters our perceptions. Research has established that social support changes our physiological and psychological responses to challenging situations. It reduces cardiovascular reactivity to stressful events and it makes the perception of physical pain less intense. When we are stressed, social support helps us more accurately assess threats rather than exaggerating them. It even changes our perception of the steepness of a hill. With a friend beside us, the hill looks easier to climb.

Social support reduces our neuroception of threat. It helps us feel safe which reduces our stress level. In adults, high levels of stress reduce our capacity for emotional and behavioral self-regulation. In children, repeated stressful experiences impair the development of emotional and behavioral self-regulation. The repeated triggering of the fight-flight-freeze stress response also interferes with the development of what psychologists call executive function skills. These are the basic cognitive skills related to completing tasks, solving problems, organizing information, and making (and revising if necessary) deliberate plans.

Many psychologists now believe that executive function is more important than intelligence in predicting a child's future academic and career success. And executive function is critical for effective social interaction. The National Scientific Council on the Developing Child tells us that children's executive function skills underpin both school achievement and children's "social, emotional, and moral development". The Council reports that "children who have problems staying focused and resisting urges to respond impulsively – two core executive function skills – not only have trouble in school but also have trouble following directions generally and are at elevated risk of displaying aggressive and confrontational behavior with adults and other children."

Two decades of research has established that the single most important factor in mitigating the effects of childhood adversity is a parent or other caregiver who consistently maintains a secure and emotionally supportive relationship with the child. A greater investment in providing physically and emotionally safe daycare, preschool, educational, and recreational environments where all children can experience stable, emotionally responsive relationships with adults would pay enormous long-term dividends in adult mental and physical health, resilience, and productivity for our nation.

Chapter 3

Motivation

If facts are the seeds that later produce knowledge and wisdom, then the emotions and the impressions of the senses are the fertile soil in which the seeds must grow.
--Rachel Carson, *The Sense of Wonder*

Years ago, I attended a freshman orientation at a struggling urban high school. A well-known motivational speaker had been flown in to speak to the students and their parents, courtesy of a local community organization, and I wanted to hear what he had to say. I was stunned when he told the students to "leave their emotions at the classroom door". I looked around at the hormone-charged adolescents and their economically challenged parents and thought: This is some of the most misguided advice I've heard in a long time.

First of all, they can't possibly do that. Secondly, emotions are critical to attention, learning, and motivation, *especially for adolescents.* We can't even make a decision without them. However purely rational we imagine our decisions to be, people who have damage to the emotional part of their brains can't make decisions. It's quite disabling. We are not like Mr. Spock.

I know what the speaker really meant; leave your poor emotional self-regulation at the classroom door. Telling students to self-regulate won't make it so, but making classrooms feel physically and emotionally safe will support their self-regulation and engagement. The best way to do that is to create a social environment in which students are connected, accepted, and feel they belong. As parents and teachers, we often see adolescents' extreme focus on their social world as an unnecessary distraction, but from an evolutionary standpoint, learning how the social world works and how to secure a place in it is a basic survival skill.

One current neuroscientific theory posits that our big brains evolved to manage the complex social relationships needed to work cooperatively in groups in the interest of survival, not to do algebra. Solving mathematical equations is a secondary advantage to our big complex brains, not their *raison d'être*. In our ancient past, anyone who found themselves isolated or rejected by the tribe was vulnerable to predators and the elements. We have a basic survival need for connection and belonging just as we do for food. And like food hunger, our hunger for connection will continue to be a distraction until the need is met. Until our schools learn to harness and utilize students' need for social connection and belonging in the service of learning, they will struggle with student motivation.

The fundamental assumptions that traditional schools make about student motivation have gone unquestioned and unchallenged for a very long time. This is in spite of the fact that research consistently shows that in the U.S., on average, students' motivation declines over the course of their school years with a large drop as they enter their middle school years. Disciplinary problems increase at this time as well.

In his book *Social: Why Our Brains are Wired to Connect*, neuroscientist Matthew Lieberman proposes that this drop in interest and academic performance in middle school is due to the fact that every student is forced to change schools at this time. All of the students go from smaller elementary schools, where they know their classmates and teachers well, to much larger schools where they have classes with students and multiple teachers they don't know. This creates an uncertain and unstable social environment that makes students feel less safe. The resulting stress reduces motivation, academic performance, and self-regulation.

Schools typically rely on the *external motivation* of rewards and punishments, A's and F's, awards, and threats of detention or a visit to the principal's office, to control and motivate students. The almost exclusive use of external rewards and punishment has failed to produce the desired results for a very long time. (Even more so in the last 20 years.) Alfie Kohn, in his book, *Punished by Rewards*, tells us that external rewards "...do not generally alter the attitudes and emotional commitments that underlie our behaviors. They do not make deep, lasting changes because they are aimed at affecting only what we do." And yet, we continue to support this failed approach. We can't imagine another way of educating our future citizens - that our children might be sufficiently curious about their world and motivated to learn without coercion. We can't fathom the possibility of schools that tap into our children's natural *internal motivation* to learn things and do things.

In elementary school classrooms, a commonly used form of external reward/punishment is to publicly display a chart with each student's name on it and an indication of the teacher's subjective assessment of each child's behavior with stars or other icons. This is a variant of the operant conditioning used by behaviorists. Everyone can see who the "bad" kids are and the "good" kids live in dread of getting the "scarlet letter" next to their name. This public humiliation or the threat of it makes students feel less emotionally safe, potentially reducing academic performance and self-regulation.

I think it's instructive to look at the behavioral theory this practice comes from. Behaviorism, as a psychological theory, began in the early 1900's but was popularized by the psychologist B.F. Skinner beginning in the 1940's. Much of the research that this behavioral approach is based on was done with rats and pigeons because Skinner believed that there was no fundamental distinction between human and animal behavior.

In behavioral theory, all behavior, no matter how complex, can be reduced to a simple stimulus-response association. And only observable behavior is relevant; thoughts and emotions are not. Educator Alfie Kohn summarizes this approach as "Do this and you'll get that." The assumption is that children and adolescents won't be motivated to learn or to comply with rules unless they are given an external incentive to do so. This assumption runs contrary to a significant body of scientific evidence that shows, in the long term, external reward/punishment schemes undermine many of the things we hope to cultivate in our children – problem solving, creativity, critical thinking, and the ability to make wise choices for themselves.

To be sure, the promise of rewards and threats of punishment can be effective in some circumstances. They can produce short term compliance for things students are already able to do, in circumstances that allow them to do it. This short-term compliance, along with discounting students' emotions, allows us to assume that this approach has long term motivational value. But if a student is unable to meet the requirements for getting the reward or avoiding the punishment, either through lack of skill or circumstances outside of their control, it can result in failure, frustration, anger, or a sense of helplessness. If I offer a sixth grader $100 to complete a series of calculus equations, she would be hugely motivated but still unable to do it. She would probably feel frustrated and angry and likely not trust me in the future because I had set her up for failure.

This applies to offering rewards for self-regulation too, as was the case for my 11-year-old client whose poor self-regulation got her in trouble at home and at school almost daily. This otherwise sweet child would fly into blind rages and afterward not remember what she had done. A therapist advised her parents to set up a behavioral chart with rewards for maintaining self-regulation. When her mother offered to buy a craft kit she had wanted for a long time, for complying with some request, the child said "No, you'll just take it away from me". This child knew she could not maintain self-regulation long enough to keep her reward.

Psychologists have long recognized the power of basic physiological needs to drive our behavior. When our needs for food, shelter, warmth, etc. are unmet, our attention and motivation are naturally diverted to doing whatever is necessary to meet them. Psychologists Edward Deci and Richard Ryan have amassed an impressive body of research to support the existence of three basic psychological needs that operate in the same way- relatedness, autonomy, and competence. They began a revolution in our understanding of human needs and motivation in the 1970's that continues to this day. As is the case with our basic physiological needs, when our basic psychological needs go unmet our attention and motivation are naturally diverted to doing whatever is necessary to meet them.

When we ignore these basic psychological needs by using behavioral approaches that rely on the external motivation of rewards and punishment to maintain student motivation and compliance, we undermine students' sense of emotional safety. Neuroscientific studies show that what Deci and Ryan call "relatedness", a sense of connection and belonging, is inherently rewarding. In brain imaging studies, positive social regard lights up our neural reward system. That's why we like the "likes" on Facebook so much. These studies show that we find cooperating with others inherently rewarding. Fairness, whether we are the ones being treated fairly or we see others treated fairly, lights up our reward system too.

Scientists tell us there are two basic types of inherent social rewards that parallel the two sides of the mother-infant relationship. The first is the reward we receive when others let us know that they like, respect, or care for us. The other reward is when we care for or treat others well.

Social connections are so critical to our wellbeing that threats to them are truly painful; social pain activates the same neural circuitry as physical pain. Social pain is real and occurs when our social bonds are threatened by rejection, alienation, disconnection, or humiliation. Social pain like physical pain is stressful and makes us feel less safe, with all the down sides that come with that. Research on social pain shows that social rejection decreases intellectual performance. We become preoccupied with our social pain which leaves fewer cognitive and attention resources for learning. Studies also show that physical pain medications like opioids relieve social pain.

In contrast, positive emotions and a sense of belonging are associated with improved thinking, decision making, and working memory. Feeling safe is a precondition to experiencing the positive emotions associated with improved academic performance. An emotionally safe school climate in which teachers and students experience social connectedness, positive regard, and a sense of fairness and belonging not only promotes better teaching and learning, it promotes better executive function and self-regulation.

One of the reasons the "do this and you'll get that" punishment /reward approach doesn't work is that it makes us feel manipulated and disempowered. It runs contrary to our basic human need for autonomy and a sense of agency. Starting around age two, toddlers' natural drive for autonomy kicks in and "no" becomes their default setting to most any request. I used to call my daughter's tantrums "autonomy storms" and just let them blow over. As our children develop, they increasingly strive for independence and greater control over their lives. This culminates in adolescents' demands for the autonomy and independent decision making they need to transition into adulthood.

Within the current constraints of our factory-like schools, students are given little autonomy and few choices in any aspect of their education. Students' time, activities, and social interactions are tightly controlled. They must even ask to use the restroom and can be refused. This control is extended into their home life through homework. In some ways, homework reduces parents' autonomy too.

How can we expect students to learn to make responsible choices and solve problems for themselves when they have so few opportunities to practice making *meaningful* choices and experience the natural (not manipulated) consequences? Problem solving is a skill that improves with practice, like a muscle that strengthens with use. Most choices offered in schools are limited to whether or not to comply with the externally imposed requirements. This does nothing to satisfy students' need for autonomy.

Research consistently shows that students have greater interest and motivation in school when they are given an opportunity to make autonomous or collaborative choices about what they are learning and doing. Making choices boosts interest and motivation whether they are made by individual students, a group of students, or a whole class. One study found that high school students who were allowed some measure of autonomy in a course in *just the first few weeks of the school year* showed increased student engagement throughout the year. This is in contrast to the decline in engagement of the students in the classrooms that didn't allow and encourage autonomy in those first few weeks.

Competence may be the basic psychological need most thwarted in our schools even though competence is the core of their mission. I have such strong feelings about this flaw in our schools that it's hard for me to write about it. Years ago, I provided therapy services at a "failing" school in rural Virginia where both the students and teachers were quite demoralized. I had a long commute with plenty of time to think. Most days I found myself crying on the way home.

I see teachers and students caught in a system that seems more focused on obedience and rating and ranking students than supporting each child's learning. Many children and adolescents feel like failures or live in fear that they will fail. My friend Jean's son is an intelligent and creative child but he has a learning disability that interferes with his academic performance. At his high school freshman orientation, Jean found him pacing back and forth in the hall in front of his math classroom door muttering "I am so stupid; I am so stupid." over and over again. Our current approach to educating children creates so much unnecessary fear of failure and shame. In *The Ecology of Learning: Re-Inventing Schools*, I devote an entire chapter to the issue of shame in learning and education.

The opportunity to exercise autonomous decision making and demonstrate competence in some endeavor, leads to what psychologists call "self-efficacy." Self-efficacy is the sense of being captain of one's own ship, capable of navigating in the world and meeting life's challenges. Successfully meeting challenges in any area of life helps buffer us from the negative effects of failure in other areas. It gives us a sense of agency- that we can make things happen in our lives. The opposite of agency is what psychologist Martin Seligman calls "learned helplessness". He explains that learned helplessness is a giving-up reaction and is "at the core of defeat and failure."

In his research, Seligman found that helplessness "...was caused by experience in which subjects learned that nothing they did mattered and that their responses didn't work to bring them what they wanted. This experience taught them to expect that in the future and in new situations, their reactions would once again be futile." Learned helplessness is a common response in students who are prevented from exercising autonomy or gaining the competence needed to succeed.

Until schools shift away from external reward/punishment motivational strategies to approaches that systematically support student's needs for relatedness, autonomy, and competence, many students will not feel emotionally safe enough to be fully engaged and motivated. This is especially true for students who are experiencing high levels of stress. There is no way to know how many students in a school fall into that category but we do know that, as a group, students living in poverty are at risk for higher levels of adversity, trauma, and toxic stress.

Seventeen percent of children in the U.S. live below the federal poverty line. During the 2016-17 school year 1.36 million enrolled students experienced homelessness at some point. Every year, more than 400,000 neglected or abused children are taken away from family members and placed with foster families. More than 50% of the children served by Head Start preschool programs have an ACE score of 3 or more adverse childhood experiences. It's estimated that about 5 million children have experienced the incarceration of a residential parent. And approximately 50% of children in the U.S. will experience the divorce or separation of their parents.

These numbers are just the tip of the iceberg. There are so many things in children's lives that can produce toxic stress. Some of the adversity students may carry with them into the classroom are emotional, physical, and sexual abuse; witnessing domestic violence; physical or emotional neglect; serious injury or illness; exposure to neighborhood violence; discrimination; a family member with mental illness or drug or alcohol addiction; property loss or damage from a fire, burglary, or natural disaster; or having a family member become seriously ill, injured, incarcerated, hospitalized, or die.

Common effects of this trauma or toxic stress are poor self-regulation, trouble forming relationships with teachers, misinterpreting things negatively, hypervigilance, and poor executive function. All of these can contribute to low academic performance and they can get students in trouble. Students who have experienced high levels of adversity are suspended and expelled at much higher rates. The traditional reward and punishment approach to school discipline is not particularly effective with their less stressed peers but it is spectacularly ineffective with students who have experienced toxic stress or trauma.

One of the reasons threats of punishment are not effective at constraining the behavior of stressed students is that toxic stress and trauma alter neuroception, the process that automatically and *unconsciously* determines whether or not situations and people are safe. Faulty neuroception can cause students to misinterpret the intentions and actions of teachers and peers as threatening and trigger a defensive fight-flight-freeze response. Threatening to punish students who already feel threatened is a prescription for disaster. We are all neurologically programmed to disengage our rational thinking, social engagement system, and our problem solving when we feel threatened. And the negative emotions that accompany the fight-flight-freeze state, such as anger or irritability, are likely to be overwhelming.

This is not a state in which a student can be expected to rationally consider potential rewards and punishments and regulate their behavior accordingly. As international trauma expert Dr. Bessel van der Kolk observes, "Despite the well-documented effects of anger, fear, and anxiety on the ability to reason, many programs continue to ignore the need to engage the safety system of the brain before trying to promote new ways of thinking."

There is a growing awareness among educators and mental health professionals of the impact toxic stress and trauma have on academic achievement, motivation, and school discipline. I see three promising efforts toward making schools feel safer for students; the trauma-informed schools movement, the teacher evaluation/coaching system called MyTeachingPartner, and the restorative discipline movement.

The trauma-informed schools movement advocates the implementation of trauma-sensitive school approaches by administrators, teachers, and staff. Trauma-informed schools reduce the effects of trauma on children by recognizing trauma responses, accommodating and responding to traumatized students within the classroom, and referring children to outside professionals when necessary. The Every Student Succeeds Act (ESSA), federal education legislation passed in 2016, has explicit provisions for trauma-informed approaches in student support, academic enrichment, and in preparing and training school personnel. According to the National Association of School Psychologists, trauma-informed schools promote feelings of physical, social, and emotional safety in students and positive culturally responsive discipline policies and practices.

The quality of student-teacher interactions is critical to students' sense of emotional safety and learning. MyTeachingPartner (MTP) is a system of professional development based on research evidence that uses teacher coaching to improve the quality of teachers' interactions with their students. It's aimed at enhancing student motivation, reducing problematic social and behavioral outcomes, and increasing student achievement. Studies on MTP have demonstrated its effectiveness in raising achievement, promoting positive peer interactions, and reducing racial disparities in teachers' discipline practices. One study found that MTP improved student performance on standardized achievement tests the equivalent of moving the average student from the 50th percentile to the 59th percentile. This improvement occurred on standardized achievement tests in English, math, social studies, and science in middle and high school students without changes in curriculum.

The restorative discipline movement seeks to promote a more relational approach to building a positive school community and addressing student behavior in order to embed true safety in schools. Restorative discipline practices foster belonging over exclusion, social engagement over control, and meaningful accountability over punishment. These practices replace reward and punishment as motivators with belonging, connectedness and the willingness to change because people matter to each other. It serves as prevention as well as intervention, with students taking more responsibility for resolving conflicts and repairing harm.

Attorney Sylvia Clute developed the Richmond Model of Restorative Justice which was first implemented in a Richmond, Virginia high school. She says the restorative discipline movement is about changing the school culture away from zero tolerance for rule breaking and the harsh exclusionary suspension and expulsion punitive practices that feed the school-to prison pipeline, to one of accountability through addressing the root causes of rule breaking. The movement seeks to "transition from a system that depends on punishment as the means to achieve compliance to a system that achieves social safety and well-being through connection, experientially learning internal control, and recognition of our shared humanity."

Clute's approach to restorative discipline uses what are called "circle" processes to provide a space where it is safe for students, teachers, and administrators to speak openly and honestly. Through the circle process, each participant contributes to identifying the root causes that fueled the conflict or rule breaking and acknowledge their role in it. Each participant identifies what they can do, with the resources they now possess, to address the causes of the conflict. Together, they can then create a mutually beneficial resolution.

In the Richmond Model Restorative Justice circle process, it's not others imposing accountability on students, as it is in a strictly punitive system, it's self-accountability. Clute gave this example of a restorative circle she facilitated with a high school student who had been disruptive. The student, we'll call Thomas, cursed, walked out of class, and slammed the door. In response, the teacher initiated a circle. In the Richmond model, everyone in the system can initiate a circle which includes a trained circle facilitator. Clute told me, "We're empowering the students to initiate circles. We're telling them, yes, you can take responsibility. And we're giving you a place where you can do that, where it's safe to be honest."

"During the circle it became clear that Thomas was very angry that the teacher made him sit in the front row. When I asked the teacher, why is it important to you that he sit in the front row, he (the teacher) said, 'Because when he sat in the back, he pulled all the stuff off my bulletin board, and besides, I need to see that he does his work.' So, we used reflective listening. I asked Thomas, what did you hear him say? And he grumbled, 'Yeah, I pulled his stuff off his bulletin board, and he wants me to do my work'. So, then I said to Thomas, why is it important to you to sit on the back row. He said, 'Because I live in a group home; I've been in detention; and when I can't see who's behind me bad things happen.' So I said to the teacher, 'What did you hear him say?' The teacher said, 'I heard him say he doesn't feel safe in my classroom'."

Clute says this is the mutual understanding they are going for in the circle process. "We want to know where everyone was in the underlying brokenness, because we're all in it. The teacher now saw what he was doing. And at that point, he knew what he could do to change that. And then the teacher said, 'Well, this is what I'll do. I'll see that you always have a seat in my classroom where you feel safe. And I want you to do your work.' And what do you think Thomas said? He said: 'Okay'."

An internal motivation to learn is critical to the life-long learning required to thrive in the 21st century economy. We have the knowledge and tools to create schools in which the seeds of internal motivation are planted by meeting students' need for safe and trusting relationships, autonomy, and competence. The question is, do we have the motivation to plant them?

Chapter 4

Crime

People who feel safe and meaningfully connected with others have little reason to squander their lives doing drugs or staring numbly at television; they don't feel compelled to assault their fellow human beings. However, if nothing they do seems to make a difference, they feel trapped and become susceptible to the lure of pills, gang leaders, extremist religions, or violent political movements – anybody and anything that promises relief.

- Bessel van der Kolk, *The Body Keeps the Score*

Our country has the highest incarceration rate in the world with 2.2 million people in the nation's prisons and jails. Americans account for around 5% of the world's population but nearly 25% of its prisoners. This is in spite of the fact that both violent and property crime have fallen sharply over the past two decades and substantial evidence that large-scale incarceration is not an effective means of achieving public safety. According to the FBI, between 1993 and 2017 the violent crime rate fell 49% and property crime fell by 50%.

It makes intuitive sense that giving criminals long mandatory sentences would serve to deter criminal behavior and lead to safer streets. Politicians over the years have appealed to this and played on our fears with "tough on crime" rhetoric to get our votes. But studies show that locking people up for long periods of time is ineffective at deterring crime, especially youth crime.

According to the U.S. Department of Justice, more than 728,000 minors were arrested in 2018. Approximately 75 percent of jailed youth are held for nonviolent charges and what are called "status offenses." Status offenses are acts that would not be a crime if they were committed by an adult. It's their "status" as a minor that makes their behavior a crime.

Status offenses include truancy, running away from home, violating curfew, underage use of alcohol and tobacco, and what they call "ungovernability". They criminalize the fight-flight-freeze behaviors of adolescents, so it's not surprising that youth incarcerated for these things are more likely to have experienced toxic stress, trauma, or be diagnosed with a mental illness. Truancy is the most common status offense. Running away from home is the only status offense committed more often by girls. These runaway adolescent girls are often escaping emotional, physical, or sexual abuse in their homes, yet they're likely to end up in custody rather than receive the services they need.

A 2019 Los Angeles County Department of Mental health investigation on the use of force and pepper spray in the county's juvenile justice system found that 91.3 percent of the youth in LA County's juvenile facilities have been diagnosed with some kind of significant mental health challenge. The report goes on to say that, "Such youth may also suffer from suicidal thinking, engage in self-injurious and/or aggressive behavior, and have a higher risk of repeat involvement in juvenile corrections. In addition, youth currently detained in juvenile halls are more likely to have experienced commercial sexual exploitation, homelessness, and a variety of other severe stressors and/or traumas, which can cause new or exacerbate underlying mental health issues."

Relatively few states define status offenses as criminal behavior under statute, yet many youth offenders like runaways or students charged with disorderly conduct for breaking school rules wind up behind bars because they violate the conditions of their probation. Standard probation conditions include regularly attending school, abiding by a curfew, not using alcohol or drugs, attending supervision appointments, and participating in mental health or other mandated services. Without family support, financial resources, transportation, and adult capacity for executive function including self-control, many youth are set up for violating these conditions and subsequent incarceration.

There's an overwhelming body of evidence showing that the wholesale incarceration of juvenile offenders does not make the public safer and youth who have been locked up are more likely to get in trouble again. A report by the Annie E. Casey Foundation concluded: "The case against America's youth prisons and correctional training schools can be neatly summarized in six words: dangerous, ineffective, unnecessary, obsolete, wasteful, and inadequate."

Widespread physical and sexual abuse, excessive use of force, and overreliance on isolation and restraint in our juvenile corrections institutions is well documented. A review of Ohio's youth correction facilities found that in July 2009, incarcerated youth spent 66,023 hours in isolation - an average of more than 50 hours per resident in one month. The impact of this trauma on the adult lives of these children is predictable but incalculable.

Educational researchers have found that upwards of 40 percent of incarcerated youth have a learning disability, and they will face significant challenges returning to school after they leave detention. Juvenile incarceration significantly reduces the likelihood of high school completion and increases the probability of incarceration later in life. Economists have shown that the process of incarcerating youth will reduce their future earnings and their ability to remain in the workforce, and could change formerly detained youth into less stable employees. Information about arrests, formal charges, and adjudications in juvenile court, which can now be accessed on-line by employers, college admission officers, consumer reporting agencies and others, can sharply limit opportunities for a lifetime.

Rodney Robinson, the 2019 National Teacher of the Year, teaches at a juvenile detention center in Richmond, Virginia. He says, "My kids are in survival mode 24/7 ... you have to show them that you care about what's going on, and then you'll be able to get them to learn." Robinson is using his platform this year to lead a conversation about the students he calls "the most vulnerable in society" and how the nation can address the school-to-prison-pipeline that has pushed too many kids out of school.

The school-to-prison pipeline should really be called the preschool to prison pipeline and it's fueled by toxic stress, trauma, and inequality. A large body of evidence supports the conclusion that, compared with otherwise similar white peers and for similar infractions, black students are suspended more frequently, for longer periods of time, and receive greater punishment. An African American student from a middle-class family is 16 percent more likely to be suspended than a white middle-class student from the same school and grade level for breaking the same school rules.

Discipline of black children is more frequently accompanied by the use of metal detectors, random searches, and/or school resource officers, none of which are consistent with a supportive learning environment. These measures are part of a trend toward zero tolerance school policies and criminalizing student behavior. Increasingly students are arrested for doing things that traditionally have been matters of school discipline and are within developmentally expected adolescent behavior. In 2019, a Kansas middle school student was arrested by a school resource officer and charged with a felony after making the shape of a gun with her fingers and pointing it at others. Actually, bringing a gun to school would just be a misdemeanor.

At least 22 states have what are called disturbing-school laws and others use disorderly conduct laws to arrest students for misbehaving in class. The presence of school resource officers in many schools, police specifically assigned to the school, make it easy for school personnel to call on them for matters that would otherwise be handled by teachers and administrators.

Police have broad discretion in determining what constitutes disorderly conduct and students have been arrested for talking back to teachers, skipping class, throwing spitballs, using profanity, refusal to take a cell phone out of a pocket, yelling in class, farting, fidgeting, being late, and having untied shoes. Suspended students who show up at schools have been charged with trespassing. In 2016, a federal appeals court upheld a school police officer's decision to arrest and handcuff a 13-year-old for disrupting a gym class by repeatedly burping. Authorities charge juveniles with some version of disturbing school more than 10,000 times a year.

The trauma and humiliation of being handcuffed and led away in front of teachers and students makes returning to school less likely for these students even if the charges are dropped. Regardless of GPA, race, or prior offenses, students who have been arrested are nearly twice as likely as their peers to drop out of high school, even if they never go to court. Students who get arrested and appear in court are nearly four times as likely to drop out of school. The greatest levels of racial disparity in the use of detention are found for the *least serious offenses*. Black students and white students are arrested for real crimes like weapons, drugs, or assault at about the same rates.

In an echo of the original Adverse Childhood Experiences research, a recent study with 14,700 adult participants found that more than 20 percent of people who had been incarcerated as children reported the worse health outcomes, including general health, functional limitations (climbing stairs), depressive symptoms, and suicidality. This compared with 13 percent for those incarcerated later in life and 8 percent for those never incarcerated.

There is a saying, "crime is a young man's game" because people tend to age out of crime. Research shows that crime starts to peak in the mid- to-late teenage years and begins to decline when individuals are in their mid-20s. After that, crime drops sharply as adults reach their 30s and 40s. The key to making our communities safer is preventing juvenile crime.

Scientists have learned a lot about adolescence in the last 30 years, including that it lasts longer than we thought, roughly from ages 12 to 24. The biological reason for extending adolescence is that important brain structures involved in executive function, including self-regulation, don't fully mature until the mid-twenties. The social reason for the extension of adolescence is the need for post-secondary education or technical training after high school to be competitive in the job market.

It's not a coincidence that this extended period of adolescence is exactly the age range with the highest crime rate. The impulsiveness and propensity for risk-taking characteristic of adolescence is a primary contributor to juvenile crime. Neuroscientists tell us this heightened risk-taking is the result of a maturational imbalance between two different brain systems. The reward centers of adolescents' brains show increased sensitivity and motivation for novelty, excitement, and sensation seeking. This makes them more prone to boredom, impulsivity, and over-valuing potential rewards while underestimating the potential risks of their choices.

The cognitive control system that counterbalances risk-taking, the one that's responsible for self-regulation and inhibiting impulses, steadily matures throughout adolescence, but is not fully developed until the late 20's. This is the executive function system involved in complicated decision-making, thinking ahead, planning, and comparing risks and rewards. Adolescence is a time of heightened vulnerability to risky and reckless behavior due to the differing maturational timetables of these two brain systems. Children who experience trauma and other adversity are at greater risk for incarceration because toxic stress impairs self-regulation by inhibiting this cognitive control system.

Changes in the brain's reward system during adolescence make this a period of social and emotional intensity too. An enhanced sensitivity to rewards makes social connection and a sense of belonging more rewarding and motivating than it is for either children or adults. Issues of identity, autonomy, and sexuality are paramount in adolescence as they seek independence and push away from parents. The strong need for bonding and belonging to a peer group makes youth more vulnerable to peer pressure and the social pain that comes with rejection. The opinions and judgements of friends rather than parents become central to adolescents' sense of self. How many times have you heard parents say, "I don't know anything since my child has become a teenager."?

It's not surprising then that researchers have found adolescents are more likely to take risks in the presence of their peers. Neuroscientists think that teenagers are more sensitive to social rewards when they are with their friends. Most of us, looking back at our youth, can see that this was the case for our own risky behavior. Furthermore, youth are more inclined than adults to commit crimes in groups.

In his book, *Brainstorm: The Power and Purpose of the Teenage Brain*, psychiatrist Dan Siegel urges us to see the up side as well as the down side of the adolescent mind. Changes in their reward systems that lead to a low threshold for boredom and novelty seeking can lead to a greater openness to change and an exuberance for life. In the right circumstances, this gives youth an advantage for creative exploration and a passion for designing new ways of doing things. Instead of settling for the status quo, they are driven toward "outside-the-box" strategies and innovation. They have a natural entrepreneurial spirit with its inherent risk taking.

Adolescents' enhanced need for connection with their peers and sense of belonging can lead them to develop the kind of close supportive relationships that increases their resilience in the face of adversity. It also makes them more inclined to work collaboratively with others for the greater good. With this innate idealism, adolescents and young adults who are given the right support, encouragement, and resources, have the potential to help us go beyond our default settings to create a more sustainable society.

Preventing juvenile crime will require us to understand and work with the psychosocial needs and strengths of adolescents and young adults, mitigating the downsides and capitalizing on the upsides. It will also require dismantling the school-to-prison pipeline. Creating a more supportive trauma-informed school climate and adopting restorative discipline practices are a necessary but insufficient step in this process. We must also make fundamental changes in the way students are taught—in pedagogy.

Pedagogy is an old-fashioned sounding word and certainly it has been absent from our modern discourse on education. It's been replaced by terms and ideas borrowed from the world of business management, most notably "management by objectives." Pedagogy refers to the interactions among teachers, students, the learning environment, and the learning tasks. It includes how teachers and students relate together and the instructional approaches implemented in the classroom. It does not include the specific content being taught but rather *how* it is taught.

The lack of concern for *how* students are taught has created much of the failure in the current business standards-driven education model with its emphasis on high-stakes testing. The basic features of this model are an established grade-by-grade set of standards, tests tied directly to those standards, and a system of rewards and punishments for teachers tied to test scores. The assumption is that if we hold teachers accountable for raising test scores, they will be motivated to do so and that it is *motivation* that teachers have been lacking. This is a basic behavioral strategy, with the classroom as a black box. The inputs are the standards, the outputs are the test scores, and the assumption is that, if motivated, teachers will change what they are doing in the black box to get the reward or avoid punishment. But what if most teachers don't know how to teach the low performing students?

Critics of Management by Objectives (MBO) argue that setting particular goals like production targets (test scores) and tying them to incentives, leads workers (teachers) to meet those targets by any means necessary, including short-cuts that result in poor quality. This is exactly what we have seen in Atlanta, Richmond, and other cities where administrators and teachers have been caught changing students' answers on high-stakes tests or giving students the test questions in advance.

Not knowing how to teach low performing students but being held accountable for doing so has led to cheating on graduation rates too. The most high-profile case of graduation-rate cheating was at Ballou High School in Washington DC. An investigation revealed that two months before graduation, only 57 students were on track to graduate, with dozens of students missing graduation requirements or failing classes needed to graduate. In June, 164 students received diplomas and the school proudly reported that all had been accepted to college. In reality, one in five of the graduates had been absent from school more than present and were not eligible to graduate.

There are other consequences to the business standards-driven education model. In survey after survey, teachers report they are stressed and demoralized and they leave the profession at a significantly higher rate than other professions. About one third of all new teachers leave education within the first five years of their teaching career.

In an article published in *Harvard Business Review*, psychologist Harry Levinson offers this criticism of Management by Objectives: "The typical MBO effort perpetuates and intensifies hostility, resentment, and distrust between a manager and subordinates. [It] fails to take adequately into account the deeper emotional components of motivation." The current business standards-driven model in our schools deprives teachers, students, and administrators of the basic drivers of motivation- relationship, autonomy, and competence. In their book, *Demoralized: Why Teachers Leave the Profession They Love and How They Can Stay*, Doris Santoro and David Berliner tell us high-stakes testing, punitive accountability systems, the narrowing curriculum, and other policies have eroded the "moral rewards" of teaching.

The myopic focus on raising test scores has led to a narrowing of the curriculum and increased "teaching to the test." The current system, including its pedagogical black box, doesn't serve any of our children well; including those who get good grades. Many students who have passed the state-mandated standardized tests required to receive their high school diplomas, graduated, and been accepted into college have not been prepared for college-level work. Across the country, millions of students enroll in college every year only to learn that they need to take remedial classes in English, math, or both before they can enroll in college level courses. Depending on the selectiveness and type of school, anywhere from 40 percent to 60 percent of first-year college students require remediation. These courses don't count toward graduation and they cost students and their families about $1.3 billion every year. Improving public K-12 education would be a much wiser investment.

According to the National Student Clearinghouse Research Center, on average just 58% of U.S. students who had started college in the fall of 2012 earned any degree six years later. Only about 16% of low-income college students graduate within 6 years. Many will be saddled with high student debt without the earning potential to pay it off, and they're more likely to end up in default.

Clearly the college and career readiness that our public elementary and secondary schools tout as their goal is not being achieved. Setting educational goals and ignoring the pedagogy, the instructional methods, needed to achieve them is not working. Part of the problem is that if teachers and administrators want to shift to more effective research evidence-based instructional approaches they are pretty much on their own. There are few established systematic processes by which more effective pedagogical approaches can be evaluated and incorporated system wide.

Research shows that approaches such as inquiry-based and project learning produce deeper learning, critical thinking, and improve executive function. They are also shown to increase student motivation and information literacy. In the 21st century, with so much information available at our finger tips, instead of requiring students to memorize and regurgitate facts and concepts, it's imperative that schools adopt instructional methods that give students information literacy– the ability to recognize when and what information is needed and to locate, evaluate, and use that information effectively.

Other professions, such as medicine, have incorporated new evidence-based practices into patient care. Mechanisms for doing this for the teaching profession must be established if we are to fully engage students and educate our next generation of citizens. My recommendation is that State Departments of Education and publicly funded state colleges and universities collaborate to establish a mechanism for systematically translating the best evidence-based teaching practices into teacher training, professional development, administrative support, and teacher evaluation.

At-risk youth need support, guidance, and opportunities outside the classroom too. National Teacher of the Year Rodney Robinson says he sees "...some of the worst basketball games you'll ever see" at the juvenile detention center where he teaches. And that "We need more programs if we want to keep our kids off the streets and active and productive and out of the prison pipeline. We get horrible basketball games because we get kids that were never taught how to play basketball." To transition into productive and fulfilling adult lives, at-risk youth need community support beyond the boundaries of schools.

Scientific studies have found that physical exercise, sports, and more complex mentally challenging tasks support the development of self-regulation and build executive function skills. These are the cognitive skills that enable us to control impulses, plan ahead, focus attention, remember instructions, and juggle multiple tasks. Executive function is the foundation of success in school and the work place.

Sports, recreational activities, art, music, and community volunteer work support the development of executive function skills and self-regulation. They also help meet adolescent's strong need for novelty that, if unmet, can lead to risk-taking. Boredom is a significant contributing factor in juvenile crime. Giving adolescents and young adults the opportunity to follow their interests, learn, and connect with peers and potential mentors outside of school can reduce their boredom, increase connection, and build skills. And research shows that youth are more willing to participate in activities *not* associated with school.

Out-of-school time activities are the surest way to meet adolescents' needs for relationship, autonomy, and competence. Through extracurricular activities youth can build skills, confidence, and a sense of self-efficacy without the pressure of tests and grades. Successfully meeting challenges in any area of life helps buffer us from the negative effects of failure in others. It gives us a sense of agency- that we can "make things happen" in our lives.

As adolescents seek independence from their parents, they look to their peers for social support, connection and belonging. Decades of studies have consistently shown that friends are more important to us and our sense of wellbeing during adolescence than any other stage of life. This is borne out for most of us when we think back to our own high school experiences. Being accepted and fitting in is so important to adolescents that they will go to extreme, often ridiculous, and sometimes dangerous lengths for peer approval. Organized activities not connected to schools offer the opportunity for adults to create safe social environments in which youth can feel connected, accepted, and that they belong. My former client, Elaine, "found" herself and her tribe when she got involved with hoop dancing. Through this activity, Elaine experienced acceptance and belonging with a peer group for the first time in her life.

The investment of time and money in athletic and enrichment activities by upper-middle-class parents for their children is increasing at the same time these "pay-to-play" activities are becoming out of reach for many middle- and low-income families. One study found that children from low-income families are half as likely to play sports as children from homes with higher incomes. Money is a barrier to participation in out-of-school time activities in another way. Most city and county parks and recreation departments don't have the budgets to support the enrichment, recreational, and athletic activities that our children need.

Community service and youth employment opportunities are another way to support the development of executive function skills and the "soft skills" that employers demand like team work, effective conflict resolution, and personal responsibility. Summer jobs programs offer a paycheck, employment experiences, and learning opportunities that can give young people a sense of pride and develop valuable work skills. Research shows that summer jobs programs reduce violence, incarceration, and mortality and they improve academic outcomes for at least a year after the end of the summer job.

I spoke to community activist Art Burton about the Richmond Urban Conservation Corps, a program he founded to employ youth to create community gardens and maintain green spaces in one of the most dangerous public housing projects in Richmond. The Corps was unique in that it combined community service with the opportunity to earn a small stipend.

"I was funded for 10 kids and 50 kids showed up" he told me. "So, my first responsibility was to figure out, how do I get rid of 40 kids? The adult community leaders had said, 'No children are going to come.' The opposite happened- 50 showed up. So, I said to the 50, I need y'all to run a mile every day. And they ran. So, I said, I need you to do jumping jacks and run a mile, the next day. And they ran and they did the jumping jacks. And then I said, I need y'all to do drill formation, jumping jacks, and run a mile and they still did it. And then the amazing part of it was some of the adults came out and started doing jumping jacks with them. At the end of two weeks, I still had 35 children and so I kept them all. All 35."

Burton said that later, after the Corps had been going for a while, a woman came up and whispered to him, "You know, I hear the people say that you're not doing anything and that you're only in it for the money, but I just want you to know that the kids you are working with are the worst kids in the neighborhood. They have been terrorizing us. They were terrorizing us before you got here and now that you're here we all's getting to sleep at night. And the kids are not that much of a problem. And she walked away."

It is time, not just to increase our investment in education, out-of-school programs, opportunities for community service, and jobs programs, but to invest more wisely in ways that produce better outcomes. This investment would pay enormous dividends in safer communities, reduced spending on law enforcement, and a more productive workforce. In the absence of this investment, we will continue to pay the price of crime and despair.

Chapter 5

Scarcity

*People can learn to control and change their behavior,
but only if they feel safe enough to experiment with new
solutions.*
- Bessel van der Kolk, *The Body Keeps the Score*

Many of us learned about the famous "marshmallow test" in undergraduate psychology classes or in the popular press. To study children's self-control, psychologist Walter Mischel and his colleagues asked preschoolers to sit alone in a room with a single marshmallow placed on table in front of them. They were told that if they could resist the temptation to eat the marshmallow for a certain amount of time, they would receive two instead of one. Follow-up of these children as adolescents found that those who had shown better self-control by waiting to get two marshmallows as children tended to have better academic achievement and life success compared to those who didn't wait. What followed from this research were efforts to teach self-control or, in some quarters, the belief that willpower was an inborn character trait that predicted future success.

A new study published in 2018 by Tyler Watts and his colleagues, replicating the marshmallow test with a much larger more diverse group of subjects found that the capacity to hold out for a second marshmallow is shaped, in large part, by a child's social and economic background. It is the child's economic and other family circumstances that affects both their ability to delay gratification and long-term success.

If we think about it, that poor children would have more difficulty resisting the marshmallow than more affluent children makes intuitive sense. For poor children and adults, financial constraints mean that the opportunity to get something they want may not come again. There is a risk that comes with waiting.

We know that children raised in poverty and other adversity are at risk for having less self-control than their more affluent peers, even in adulthood. But in their book *Scarcity: Why Having Too Little Means So Much,* Harvard economist Sendhil Mullainathan and Princeton psychologist Eldar Shafir explain that even adults who experienced very little adversity as children, show a reduction in their self-control and executive function skills when they encounter circumstances of scarcity of money or time. Mullainathan and Shafir define scarcity as the *perception* of having more needs than resources and they tell us this scarcity mind set comes with a cognitive tax.

One of the features of the scarcity cognitive tax is a narrowing of focus they call "tunneling." Scarcity captures our attention and pushes out thoughts irrelevant to meeting our unfulfilled needs. We unconsciously neglect things outside our scarcity tunnel. I see how this works in my own life. When I'm in a time-crunch tunnel, I'm more likely to lose things, forget appointments, and not take out the garbage. It's not that we consciously choose to neglect other possibly more important things, rather, they don't even come to mind.

Most of us have experienced tunneling when we've been preoccupied with an important deadline or a serious health or money problem. Thinking back, we may have regrets about neglecting things or people outside our scarcity tunnel. Tunneling helps explain why the poor are less compliant about medical protocols and forget to take their medication, even without financial considerations. There can be other serious consequences to tunneling, especially for children who are often outside their parents' time-scarcity tunnel.

I think tunneling accounts for some of the tragic instances of young children being left in hot cars. In 2018, fifty-three children died as a result of being left in hot cars in the U.S. Over 50 percent of those deaths occurred because a caregiver forgot the child was in the vehicle. The National Safety Council advises parents and caregivers to put something that's more likely to be in their tunnel in the back seat with the child like a purse, briefcase or even a left shoe to force one last look before walking away.

Another cognitive tax associated with scarcity is a reduction in what Mullainathan and Shafir call mental bandwidth, a combination of executive function and cognitive capacity. Bandwidth is shorthand for the psychological mechanisms that underlie self-control and our ability to solve problems, retain information, and engage in logical reasoning- all the things that go into sound decision making.

The amazing thing is that the same person's bandwidth can change depending on their *perception* of abundance or scarcity. For example, studies show farmers in India have less bandwidth and ability to problem solve before harvest. After harvest they regain their bandwidth. I experienced this same phenomenon when, out of the blue, I received a notice from the IRS saying I owed $6,000 in corporate taxes on my therapy practice.

My bandwidth immediately plummeted and I couldn't understand their explanation of why I owed this money. There was a full explanation of it right there on the page, but I just couldn't understand it. And my bandwidth stayed diminished for another hour or so. All of this in spite of the fact that I didn't owe the IRS anything. It was just a bureaucratic error.

The cognitive tax associated with poverty sets people up for failure and perpetuates their poverty. The prevailing view is that failure causes poverty but, in fact, poverty causes failure. The poor have no financial margin for error; they can't afford to make a mistake yet the cognitive tax keeps them from thinking clearly, increasing the probability that they will make a serious mistake. And events like a car breaking down that might be an inconvenience to someone who can afford to repair it can be a disaster for someone who can't. Without transportation, job loss and eviction are very real possibilities. It's the sort of thing that can lead to homelessness.

Years ago, I interviewed Alice Tousignant, then executive director of Virginia Supported Housing, for a radio show I called "Consider the Alternative" that aired on our local independent station. One of the things that stuck with me from the interview was her answer to my question about what was new on the horizon for reducing homelessness. Tousignant described new research on homelessness that had taken a novel approach: Homeless people were asked what they needed. The "surprising" conclusion was that they needed housing!

Apparently, the prevailing theory was that homeless people "needed" to clean up their act, get sober, or avail themselves of mental health and other social services before they were *qualified* to receive permanent housing assistance. Not surprisingly, this isn't an effective approach to reducing homelessness. The research is quite clear that a sense of safety is a prerequisite to having the kind of self-control necessary to make life changes. Tousignant told me research was then underway on the efficacy of providing housing first and then wrapping the needed support services around the formerly homeless person.

Fast forward to my recent interview with Allison Bogdanovic the current executive director of Virginia Supported Housing. She told me a movement called Housing First was born out of the research Tousignant described years earlier. It showed that providing safe, secure housing first could end long-term homelessness at a much higher rate than the prevailing approach. Bogdanovic said subsequent research has shown that a Housing First approach can deliver significantly better results at a lower cost mainly due to reduced spending on emergency medical services, hospitalization, and incarceration.

Beyond the cost savings there is the heartache savings. The safety of secure housing along with medical and social support helps people rebuild their lives. Many homeless people have become estranged from their families. Bogdanovic told me one of the most gratifying aspects of her job was seeing them reconnect and repair those relationships. Among the reconnection stories she told was one of a formerly homeless woman who now babysits her grandchildren.

Homelessness is at the extreme end of the continuum of housing insecurity but many families live on the edge of that cliff because the U.S. is in the midst of an affordable housing crisis. According to the U.S. Department of Housing and Urban Development, housing is considered unaffordable if it costs more than 30% of a family's income. Beyond 30% and the family is considered "cost burdened", likely straining to make it from paycheck to paycheck with nothing left over for unexpected expenses like a sick child or a car breaking down. My friend, who grew up living on the edge of poverty, recalls the times her mom called the three siblings together just before pay day to say "Don't let nothin' happen."

Nearly half of all renters are cost burdened and 11 million Americans (roughly the population of New York City and Chicago combined) spend more than half their paycheck on rent. Home prices are rising at twice the rate of wage growth so we can expect to see an increasing number of families who don't have a safe, secure place to go home to every night. In Virginia, the minimum wage is $7.25 per hour and the average wage of a renter in Richmond is $18.27 per hour. Compare this to the $23.13 per hour needed to pay 30% of income for a modest two-bedroom apartment and you can see the magnitude of the problem just in Richmond, Virginia.

In California, New York, Hawaii, and the District of Columbia you need to make $30 per hour or higher to afford the rent on a two-bedroom apartment. Great swathes of our country are becoming unaffordable to low- and middle-income citizens. Increasingly, teachers can't afford to live in the districts where they teach. San Francisco is the poster child for this problem, but affluent districts in Colorado, Indiana, Illinois, North Carolina, Florida, New Jersey, Connecticut, and New York are considering or have implemented housing subsidies and other more creative housing assistance to try to recruit and retain teachers.

An international comparison of rental housing affordability in 12 advanced countries found the United States has the least affordable housing despite high average incomes. The analysis indicates that the greater cost burdens found among renters in the U.S. are largely due to greater income inequality and to more limited housing assistance programs.

The affordable housing crisis in the U.S. has led to an eviction crisis. Some experts say the eviction crisis is starting to look a lot like the subprime mortgage crisis. Those of us with secure housing rarely, if ever, think about eviction unless it's brought to our attention as it was for me when a neighbor down the street was evicted. I didn't know the family, but It was so sad to see their furniture piled on the front lawn of their house. The next day I had to call the county animal rescue department about their obviously well cared for but now abandoned dog. I can't imagine the level of shame, chaos, and fear that being evicted must bring to a family.

The national data on eviction is incomplete but of the cities for which statistics are available, Richmond, Virginia ranks among the highest. In 2016, about 1 in 9 renter households in Richmond were issued eviction court judgments. And one in five renter households in Richmond were threatened with eviction. The majority of these evictions occurred in segregated, mostly black neighborhoods. The median amount owed was $686.

Sociologist Matthew Desmond, author of the Pulitzer Prize winning book *Evicted: Poverty and Profit in the American City* says "Eviction isn't just a condition of poverty; it's a cause of poverty". Not only does it force families into shelters and degraded housing, eviction comes with a mark that goes on your record that can bar you from moving into decent housing in a safe neighborhood. Eviction is such a traumatic event that the vulnerability, stress, and shame reduce people's mental bandwidth and their capacity to make good decisions.

We think of job loss as a cause of eviction, but there is strong evidence that eviction contributes to job loss. The cognitive tax and unstable living arrangements that come with eviction can reduce an employee's reliability and productivity. It's hard to make it to work on time and stay focused without a safe, secure housing base. The high level of stress and poor living conditions can compromise both physical and mental health. One study found that mothers who get evicted experience high rates of depression two years later.

Housing instability has a devastating impact on children's well-being too. The stress, reduced self-control, and tunneling that parents experience as they struggle to keep a roof over their families' heads and meet other expenses while continuing to get their children to school and themselves to work can make tempers short and lead to emotional neglect or abuse. Not surprisingly, studies show that housing instability and poor-quality housing are associated with worse emotional, behavioral, and cognitive functioning in children and adolescents. Needless to say, their academic performance and classroom behavior decline.

It's hard to climb out of poverty and it's easy to fall into its downward spiral. The families and friends of most people in this situation have few resources to provide much of a safety net. And in spite of our society's belief in a meritocracy, the structural inequality built into our laws, business practices, government policies, education, health care, and the media place a powerful drag on any one person's ability to pull themselves up by the boot straps.

Current U.S. census data puts 12.3 % of the population- one in eight- below the federal poverty level; that's approximately 40 million people. One in five children live in poverty. Many of us assume low-income Americans are disproportionately from metropolitan areas but that is not the case. The poverty rate is slightly higher in rural areas than in cities.

Many experts contend that the way the federal government calculates the poverty threshold is antiquated and underestimates poverty in America. Also, being above the federal poverty threshold doesn't mean you can afford housing and other necessities, or can manage an unexpected expense any better. Given the high cost of housing, many people who live well above the poverty threshold of $25,283 for a family of four have insufficient income left to make ends meet after paying their rent. These families are just one illness, injury, car repair, or job loss away from eviction or an overwhelming burden of high interest debt.

These families are poor by any reasonable measure. They live with the daily stress of material insecurity. They don't feel safe and indeed they aren't safe. There is no net beneath the economic tight rope they walk. It is the physiological and psychological effects of the stress, of not feeling safe, that accounts for most of the well-documented negative health and social effects of poverty.

Moreover, we don't actually need to *be poor* to experience some of the psychological downsides of poverty; we only need to *feel poor* relative to others. You will recall from Mullainathan and Shafir's work that the cognitive tax and loss of bandwidth that come with scarcity are not only tied to objective scarcity but to the *perception* of scarcity. Epidemiologists Richard Wilkinson and Kate Picket have demonstrated that after a threshold of material living standards is met, it is our *perception* of how our income compares to those around us that's associated with health and social problems.

Wilkinson and Picket discovered this while doing international comparisons of a country's health and social well-being with the country's average income. As they plotted out the data, the researchers found the expected relationship of worse health and social outcomes in the more impoverished countries and better indicators of wellbeing in the countries with a higher average income. This relationship held until they looked at the wealthier developed countries and there the expected relationship ended. The better social and health indicators weren't tied to higher average income in the developed nations.

As they looked for factors that could explain the differences in health and social wellbeing among the wealthier countries, what they found was astonishing. Income inequality, the gap between the richest and the poorest people within a country, predicted the level of health and social problems in these countries. The higher a country's income inequality, the worse the health and social problems. In their books, *The Spirit Level: Why greater Equality Makes Societies Stronger* and *The Inner Level: How More Equal Societies Reduce Stress, Restore Sanity and Improve Everyone's Wellbeing,* Wilkinson and Picket explore how inequality produces these negative consequences.

Among the developed nations of Western Europe, the United States, Canada, and Japan, the U.S. has the highest average income, highest income inequality, and highest level of health and social problems. Our closest neighbors on the income inequality scale are Portugal and Britain. This relationship between income inequality and levels of health and social problems seen in international comparisons holds true when comparing individual U.S. states too. For example, the greater the income inequality in a state the shorter the life expectancy of the people living there. The impact of inequality on physical and mental health is greater for stress related conditions such as heart disease, obesity, and depression and its impact increases as you descend the income ladder.

For me, the most important take away from Wilkinson and Picket's research is the corrosive effect inequality has on community life, sense of wellbeing, and social mobility. Compared to other developed nations, Americans have the lowest social mobility – the potential for moving up the economic and social ladder and for children to do better economically than their parents. Of course, it hasn't always been this way. Social mobility increased steadily in the U.S. from 1950 to 1980. But since then, social mobility has declined dramatically with the rapidly widening gap between the rich and the poor. We are no longer the land of opportunity.

Economists Matthias Doepke and Fabrizio Zilibotti describe another widening gap produced by inequality – a parenting gap. In their book *Love, Money, and Parenting: How Economics Explains the Way we Raise Our Kids*, they describe how inequality raises the stakes in parenting and that affluent parents have responded by shifting to more intensive parenting with a greater emphasis on educational achievement to secure a higher position on the economic ladder for their children. With more economic resources and social capital to invest in their children, affluent "helicopter" parents leverage this to gain greater security and success for their children. Doepke and Zilibotti tell us that "The increase in the parenting gap further exacerbates inequality and creates a persistent barrier against social mobility."

Another downside of our growing economic inequality is the divisiveness and loss of trust within our communities. As we will see, the neuropsychological effects of such a large gap between the rich and poor reduces the quality and satisfaction we derive from our social connections. This has resulted in reduced "social capital", the networks of relationships among people who help each other and work together for mutual benefit and the common good. The rise in competition and drop in cooperation makes us all feel less safe. Many of us don't even know our neighbors. The social alienation exacerbated by inequality may account for the fact that the highest number of mass shootings in the U.S. occur in areas that combine both high levels of inequality and high levels of income.

Stress is the obvious mechanism by which poverty impacts physical health and psychological wellbeing. Its negative effects are well documented and it's easy to see how poor people don't feel safe – they aren't. But how does income inequality produce some of those same effects on those of us who are not poor? It makes us feel less safe too.

The heightened stress of living in an unequal society has its roots in two aspects of our psychological makeup. One is the neuropsychological effect of social hierarchy, and the other is our dependence on the social group for survival. Those who are lower in social rank or more subordinate have higher levels of the stress hormone cortisol than more dominant, higher ranking members of the group. It's stressful to be at the bottom of the social ladder when those above you control the material resources and can use their power to punish you.

In studies of employees of distinctively hierarchical organizations, those with lower status jobs have higher levels of cortisol than those higher on the corporate ladder. Low status employees react more strongly to stressful events with a greater increase cortisol, and it takes low status employees much longer for their cortisol level to return to baseline after stressful events. In strongly hierarchical societies, as well as organizations, our position on the social ladder determines our vulnerability to the loss of material and social support needed for survival.

The second primary contributor to the stress of inequality is that we are hardwired to need social acceptance and find it rewarding. Conversely, we find social rejection quite literally painful. Social rejection activates brain regions that are associated with both social and physical pain. No wonder the most unequal U.S. states have higher rates of drug addiction and more deaths from drug overdoses. These drugs are effective for temporarily relieving the pain of social rejection and shame.

Our fundamental survival need for acceptance and belonging makes other people's judgements of us very powerful in terms of our sense of self, safety, and wellbeing. This creates what psychologists call a "social evaluative threat" in situations where we are likely to be judged. Members of racial, ethnic, religious, and other groups for whom social rejection and discrimination are a consistent aspect of social interactions, live with the physiological and psychological consequences of the chronic stress of inequality throughout their lives. Children who are repeatedly exposed to the social rejection of discrimination experience this chronic stress as trauma with the same health and emotional consequences as other adverse childhood experiences.

The social evaluative threat is more intense in societies where material resources are distributed extremely unevenly and competitively, because the risks of being judged negatively are perceived to be higher and the perceived benefits of a positive judgement are greater. In these societies, the potential for judgement of every conceivable facet of ourselves, our background, and our relationships can make social interactions feel threatening and stressful.

Many of us experience this as social anxiety. Psychologists have coined the term "status anxiety" to explain the insecurity people feel in our increasingly competitive and hierarchical social environments. The popular media, with its fixation on status and celebrity, turn our natural tendency to compare ourselves to others into a toxic exercise in shaming and blaming ourselves and others up and down the social ladder. In such a competitive social milieu, authenticity is at a premium and it can even feel risky.

Research has shown that online social networking creates a sort of extreme peer pressure. Since most people are reluctant to post negative or upsetting experiences on Facebook, it seems like everyone is doing better and having more fun than we are. Exposure to our friends' carefully curated images can easily lead to negative self-comparison.

An underlying erroneous assumption that drives much of our status anxiety is that we are living in a *meritocracy*. We assume that people advance up the social ladder based on their individual merits and accomplishments. This assumption leads us to think that if we or they don't rise, it's our/their own fault. This is far from the truth, but it conveniently allows us to feel superior to those below us on the ladder. The flip side of this coin is that, in a meritocracy, as we compare ourselves to the images coming at us on our screens and the achievements of others lauded in the media, we have only ourselves to blame for coming up short. Our sense of self-worth is tied to our position on the ladder and how we compare to our immediate peers and distant celebrities.

Status anxiety fueled by advertising is a primary driver of the wasteful, self-defeating, and unsustainable consumerism in this country. Studies have shown that conspicuous consumption is intensified by inequality. If you live in a more unequal area, you are more likely to spend money on a flashy car and shop for status goods. The strength of this effect on consumption can be seen in the tendency for inequality to drive up levels of personal debt as people try to enhance their status. Of the 100 largest U.S. counties, those where income inequality grew most rapidly were also those that experienced the largest increases in three important symptoms of financial distress: divorce rates, long commutes, and bankruptcy filings.

Even the wealthy are not immune to status anxiety and the fear that they will lose their lofty place on the social ladder or be unable to secure that position for their children. Exhibit A for this is the 2019 "Operation Varsity Blues" college admissions bribery scandal which is still ongoing. Thirty-five wealthy parents (including some celebrities) of college applicants are accused of paying more than $25 million between 2011 and 2018 to the founder of a "college counseling" organization who organized the scheme. He guaranteed parents their children would be admitted to elite universities that they could not get into on their own merit.

To get these students into the elite schools, the organizer arranged for them to cheat on the SAT or ACT college admission tests, fabricated sports credentials for "boutique" sports like water polo and sailing, and bribed college officials. Thus far, 52 people have been indicted and charged with a range of crimes including racketeering, money laundering, obstruction of justice, wire fraud, mail fraud, and bribery.

It was not concern over the quality of their children's education that drove these parents to break the law. You can get a decent education at most of the state colleges and universities across this country. My degrees from state universities have proved to be a sound foundation for my career. No, these parents were obsessed with the status that comes from having a child in an elite school and the social connections and career opportunities that come to their child at an elite university. All of this hinges on a fundamental belief that we live in a meritocracy. Your child's admission to a highly competitive elite school, presumably on their own merits, publicly validates both their innate talent and your parenting skills. And with the lack of upward social mobility in this country, these parents were desperate to pass on their privileges to their children and avoid downward mobility at all costs.

In his book *The Meritocracy Trap: How America's Foundational Myth Feeds Inequality, Dismantles the Middle Class, and Devours the Elite*, Yale law professor Daniel Markovits tells us this incident is not an isolated one, it's just that the means the elite typically use to game the system are legal. The fact that even the wealthy are driven to such lengths to gain and maintain privilege, shows us the pervasiveness of status anxiety across the entire socioeconomic spectrum. This helps explain the high levels of stress so many of us feel, regardless of our objective circumstances, and our maladaptive attempts to cope with this stress. The profound economic and social inequality we are experiencing in this country is bankrupting us morally and robbing all of us of the social connectedness and sense of well-being that supports our physical and mental health.

We are the wealthiest country in the world. The U.S. spends more on health care per person than any other nation, yet we have the poorest physical and mental health outcomes of any of the developed nations. The stress of inequality is only part of this picture. As we will see in the next chapter, our health care system actually contributes to the inequality, increasing economic distress and the psychological stress that comes with it, thus working against its own purposes.

Chapter 6

Health

The First wealth is health.
-Ralph Waldo Emerson

The headline of the September 9, 2019 *Washington Post's* Health Section read "'UVA has ruined us': Health system sues thousands of patients, seizing paychecks and putting liens on homes". The quote is from former University of Virginia (UVA) health system patient, Heather Waldron, who was treated there in 2017 for complications from an intestinal malformation. The hospital sued her for $164,000 after she discovered her insurance had lapsed because of a computer error involving a policy she bought on healthcare.gov.

Waldron, 38, an insurance agent and former nurse, says she is now on food stamps and talking to bankruptcy lawyers. A bank began foreclosure proceedings in August on the Blacksburg, Virginia. house she shared with her husband until the financial disaster strained their marriage and contributed to their divorce. The home will be sold to pay off the mortgage. She expects UVA to take whatever is left.

The UVA health system is a taxpayer-supported and state-funded nonprofit hospital that pays no federal, state or local taxes on the presumption it offers charity care and other community benefits worth at least as much as those breaks. Over six years, the state institution filed 36,000 lawsuits against patients seeking a total of more than $106 million in unpaid bills.

In 2018, the number of people in the U.S. without health insurance rose to 27.5 million. But having insurance is no guarantee you won't get hauled into court over medical debt. Coverage limits, having a "high-deductible" plan (increasingly common coverage that can require patients to pay more than $6,000 before insurance kicks in), and what have come to be called "surprise" medical bills through inadvertently receiving care from an out-of-network provider, all add up to out-of-pocket expenses that many can ill afford. Having health insurance doesn't insure against overwhelming medical bills.

A recent study found that two-thirds of U.S. bankruptcies are connected to medical bills. Of the developed nations of the world, only the U.S. has a growing problem with medical debt and medically related bankruptcy. It is virtually unknown in other advanced countries because the U.S. is the *only* advanced nation that does not have universal affordable healthcare. As the World Health Organization defines it, "universal health coverage means that *all people* have access to the health services they need, when and where they need them, *without financial hardship.*"

There is a reason why all of the other advanced nations on earth provide some form of universal health coverage to all of their citizens. It strengthens their country socially and economically. Just as universal public education is a proven extraordinary public investment providing a more effective citizenry and a more productive workforce; universal health coverage is a wise public investment that will return far more to our national prosperity than it costs in tax dollars. Sickness is costly, it shrinks the workforce and makes it less productive. Good health, like education, expands the workforce and makes it more productive.

According to the international financial institution, World Bank, a "…growing body of evidence shows that without a healthy, educated and resilient population, countries cannot compete effectively in the global economy. When investments in health begin in the early years of life and are sustained through the life cycle, they lay a strong foundation for the growth and competitiveness of nations. Investing in health systems that ensure that all people have access quality, affordable health services so that they are healthy and productive throughout their lives– the essence of Universal Health Coverage-- is thus a key human capital investment."

All of the other countries with universal health coverage have solved the problem of how to provide their citizens with the health care they need while protecting patients from high medical costs. A key component of this is that they keep health care costs in check through regulation and negotiating with providers. Each country has solved this problem in a different way but their solutions fall into three main categories: single-payer, socialized medicine, and mandated insurance. Many countries' health systems are a hybrid of these with the politics and economics of a country impacting how they develop and implement universal health coverage. In this process, trade-offs are made so each country's plan has advantages and disadvantages.

Under a *single-payer system of universal health coverage*, everyone receives comprehensive coverage regardless of their ability to pay and the government is the "single-payer" for the coverage, not the multiplicity of health insurance corporations that we now have in the U.S. In a single-payer system, health care services are provided by private hospitals and providers but the costs are billed to the government. Medicare and Medicaid are examples of single-payer systems in the U.S. When politicians say "Medicare -for-All" they mean a single-payer system of universal health coverage.

Single-payer is the type of universal health coverage that Canada provides to its citizens. They call their system, "Medicare." In Canada's Medicare system, all hospital visits and care at the doctor's office are fully covered for everyone with no co-pays or deductibles. The cost for prescription drugs, dental, vision, and rehabilitation services are not covered so Canadians must pay for these through supplemental health insurance plans (often through employers), government programs for vulnerable individuals such as seniors, minors, and those with disabilities, or out-of-pocket. Canada has price controls for medications, so prescription drugs are far less expensive than in the U.S.

Attorney Pamela Donison moved from Arizona to Canada with her Canadian husband in large part to take advantage of Canada's Medicare system following her diagnosis and successful treatment for breast cancer. Pamela and her husband, Brian, realized they would be financially ruined if they stayed in the states and the cancer returned. Pamela's insurance covered the treatment for her breast cancer, but their out-of-pocket expenses were approximately $35,000. Included in this total was a surprise bill of $5,000 from an anesthesiologist who was out-of-network, despite having no notice or control over the choice of professional. Also included in that total are the services of a private billing expert, as recommended by the clinic providing her treatment. The clinic told her this was necessary to get maximum payment from the insurance company because "one wrong dot of the "i" and they will reject your claim." She was also advised that her particular insurer was well known for rejecting claims related to breast cancer.

Pamela's experiences with Canadian Medicare have been very different both from a cost standpoint and with her providers. Not only have her multiple doctor's office visits and one visit to the emergency room cost her nothing out-of-pocket, but she is more satisfied with the services she received. Pamela sees the Canadian system as much less fragmented and more centered around the patient. Her initial office visit was scheduled for two hours with a nurse practitioner to take a complete medical history that could then be accessed by any future medical practitioner she saw in the provincial system.

Because Pamela's blood pressure was high, the nurse practitioner referred her to a cardiologist to get baseline information on her cardio-vascular status. She was prescribed a low dose of medication and referred to a physical therapist and nutritionist to support her in making the lifestyle changes needed to manage her blood pressure. All at no charge. When Pamela remarked how different this was from her experience of health care in the U.S., they explained that Canada has adopted a more integrated community-based approach that includes prevention, public health, and primary care services.

In explaining their decision to move to Canada, Pamela told me, "Knowing that I could be a Canadian resident and eventually a citizen, and not have to impoverish my family if I needed further treatment, was a huge factor. It's the security of knowing that I can receive treatment at any time for anything at no cost other than my tax dollars. I can't even express how big that is. I don't think people in the U.S. quite grasp the impact of not having to fret over: Does my job have enough insurance? Will I be covered? Is there a waiting period, do I have 90 days where I cannot get sick or get in an accident or break my leg by falling down the stairs, you know, all of these things? It's a constant thing that sits on your shoulder. If you've ever had any sort of health insecurity, it just sits there. It's so stressful it makes every little thing bigger. With even a minor illness or injury, suddenly your mind is going but what if, but what if, but what if. It's so stressful."

In a *socialized medicine system of universal health coverage*, the government is the single-payer for health care. It owns the healthcare facilities like hospitals, and it employs the professionals who work in them. In the U.S., the Veterans Health Administration (VA) is an example of socialized medicine. All VA hospitals are owned by the government and the health care providers are all employees of the government.

Socialized medicine is the form of universal health coverage provided to citizens in Great Britain through their National Health Service (NHS). It pays for all medical care, including preventive care, hospital care (including outpatient drugs), physician services, some dental and vision, mental health, hospice care, some long-term care, rehab, and home care. There are only co-pays for prescription drugs, but they are capped at $12, no matter how expensive the medication. Private insurance coverage and private pay options are available.

I spoke with Ailsa Long, a single mother who has lived with her son Jesse on both sides of the Atlantic, about their experiences with health care in the two countries. She said that people in Britain do complain about the NHS. She feels they take it for granted. Ailsa said that, yes, there can be a wait of a day or two for non-urgent care for adults (children are seen quickly) but that the wait is a small tradeoff for knowing you will always receive care with no co-pay or other charge. She told me the care her father received for seven years for Lou Gehrig's disease would have bankrupted the family if they had been in the U.S. - "we would have lost our house and everything".

Ailsa said, "It's a safety thing... when I was in England, even though I was out of work for eight months which was terribly painful for me, I knew, getting in the car that if anything happened to me, or Jesse, we will be taken care of. And I didn't have that immense sense of doom sitting on my head, if someone should crash into me or whatever, you know." She added, "Okay, so there are the possible negative things sure, the Mental Health Services have a long way to go.... To me, the NHS system is the pulse of a community that keeps everybody alive."

A *mandated Insurance system of universal health coverage* is a bit more complex than either single-payer or socialized medicine. In it the government mandates that all citizens purchase health insurance from private or public health insurers. It often includes a requirement for a standard minimum coverage across all insurers and subsidizes insurance for low income individuals.

Germany has a mandated national social health insurance system which began with legislation passed in 1883. Health insurance is mandatory for all citizens and permanent residents of Germany. The majority of Germans are required to purchase their insurance from 118 not-for-profit highly regulated "Sickness Funds". This Statutory Health Insurance (SHI) system covers physician and preventive care, hospital, mental health, dental, vision, physical therapy and rehab, prescription drugs, medical equipment, hospice and palliative care, and sick leave.

In Germany insurance premiums are calculated as a percentage of gross wages up to a ceiling so higher earners pay more toward the common insurance fund than low wage workers, however; everyone gets the same full coverage regardless of the premium they pay. There are no deductibles, total annual cost-sharing (co-pays and out-of-pocket expenses) is capped at 2% of income. Non-earning dependents and children are covered free of charge. Unemployed people contribute to the SHI in proportion to their unemployment benefits and the government pays the insurance premiums for the long-term unemployed. Self-employed and high-income employees can choose to opt out of the SHI system and purchase private health insurance instead.

I met with Regi Franz and Lothar Pausewang, in the home of mutual friends, to discuss their experiences with the German and U.S. health care systems. Regi is Swiss but lived in Germany for several years and Lothar is German. When we met, Regi was sporting a wrist brace – the result of a recent fall. She had chosen to manage the injury to her wrist and ribs herself, rather than going to the doctor, because of the high out-of-pocket expenses under her current insurance plan. She told me "I would go to the doctor for something like this in Germany. I wouldn't think twice about it."

Lothar concurred, "people like us who are making okay money. We feel completely unsecure here. I only pray that nothing really serious will happen to me before I could join Medicare. Because even being insured, knowing all the horror stories of bills coming in you have no idea who they are from and how so you feel vulnerable because you have to fight against the system. So far, we are super lucky. And I think America is not for the faint of heart. And that's really true. I mean, you have to hope everything goes well and you stay healthy. I never had that feeling, anytime in Germany. I was not even thinking about the monetary impact of sickness. So, of course you're sick you go to the doctor, and you don't abuse the system. But I mean it's never kind of a second thought that I cannot go because I'm afraid, oh god, what will it cost. You are covered."

Critics of universal health coverage say that universal coverage would decrease Americans' freedom to choose the type of health care coverage they want. But how much choice do ordinary people really have in the current system? Only the wealthy have meaningful choices in their health insurance. And the current system of financing health care reduces Americans' freedom to make other *more important choices* in their lives.

The majority of Americans, 55 percent, are covered through employer-sponsored health insurance. One of the down sides of having health insurance tied to full-time employment is what has come to be called "job lock" - when workers are reluctant to leave a job that offers health insurance because they cannot otherwise obtain affordable insurance. Economists say job lock distorts the labor market and makes it less efficient in a number of ways. The need for health insurance, may keep workers stuck in jobs that do not fully use their skills or allow for career advancement, or that provide an unpleasant workplace environment. Workers who have serious health problems or have family members with serious health problems are particularly likely to be locked into jobs because of insurance concerns.

Job lock causes many workers to stay employed (or employed full-time) when it would otherwise be in their best interest to work part-time, take a hiatus from the work place, or retire. I know several mothers who would prefer to work part-time or stay home with their young children, but their husbands are self-employed so these women must work full-time to secure insurance benefits for the family. Job lock can prevent individuals from reducing their hours to care for family members, further their education, follow their dreams, or to move gradually toward retirement.

Job lock also discourages entrepreneurship. Starting a business is always a risky proposition, but having to do so without insurance adds another major element of risk. Access to insurance outside of employment reduces the risk and increases the probability that workers would leave jobs to start their own businesses. Some economists predict that decoupling health insurance from employment would be good for the small businesses that account for 49 percent of all private-sector employment in this country. Right now, employers with less than fifty full-time employees are not required to provide group health insurance coverage to their employees and most choose not to, due to the high cost. This makes it harder to attract and retain high quality workers. Universal health coverage could unlock entrepreneurship, produce a much more fluid labor market, and give greater security to workers in the gig economy.

Universal health coverage decreases inequality and would increase the sense of safety and security for middle and low-income Americans. Employer-sponsored health insurance is generally not available for part-time employees and many low wage workers cannot afford the insurance offered by their employer or can only afford a high deductible plan. Research shows that when low-income Americans have affordable health insurance, it improves their overall economic wellbeing as well as their health. Multiple studies comparing states that expanded Medicaid coverage for low-income people with states that did not, found large improvements in financial health in states with expanded coverage including significant reduction of poverty rates.

Medicaid expansion was associated with reductions in unpaid bills, over limit credit card spending, medical bills, delinquencies, bankruptcies, and payday loan debt. Providing low-income families with health insurance led to fewer evictions per month with the most pronounced reduction in evictions in counties with high rates of uninsured residents before the expansion. The researchers conclude that "Medicaid not only is an important part of the health care safety net but also may be considered a key strategy for addressing poverty-related housing instability."

In an analysis of health insurance and income inequality, economists Robert Kaestner and Darren Lubotsky conclude that Medicare and Medicaid *decrease inequality* and that Employer Sponsored Health Insurance *increases inequality*. The lack of equity in employer-based health insurance is largely due to the fact that workers with high paid jobs get most of the benefits. As health costs rise, enrollees in employer plans face higher out-of-pocket healthcare spending both through rising premium contributions and increased co-pays and deductibles when they use services.

For most of those with employer coverage, the cost of the premium is split between the employer and employee. The employer's portion is exempt from federal income and payroll taxes. This tax exclusion amounts to a federal government subsidy of employer sponsored health insurance and is the government's third largest expenditure on health care, after Medicare and Medicaid. This government subsidy contributes to income inequality because it goes to higher income individuals who have employer sponsored health insurance – the people who need it the least.

Paying for health care through taxes as in Canada and Great Britain or as a percent of wages into a Sickness Fund as in Germany, instead of through insurance premiums and deductibles, makes health care financing much more equitable. There, in hard times, people pay less and in good times they pay more. Either way, the people in those countries always have health insurance. In our current system, when someone loses their job, becomes seriously ill, or is injured, the potential financial hardship of medical bills they can't pay significantly adds to their stress. Universal health coverage would improve the physical, mental, and financial health of all but the most affluent in our country.

It is time for us to join the other advanced nations of the world in providing affordable health care to all of our citizens. It is the single most important step we can take to reduce the effects of income inequality, restore social mobility, and increase the sense of safety and well-being for all Americans.

Appendix

What's Your ACE Score?

https://acestoohigh.com/got-your-ace-score/

The most important thing to remember is that the ACE score is meant as a guideline: If you experienced other types of toxic stress over months or years, then those would likely increase your risk of health consequences.

Prior to your 18th birthday:

Did a parent or other adult in the household often or very often... Swear at you, insult you, put you down, or humiliate you? or Act in a way that made you afraid that you might be physically hurt?

   No___If Yes, enter 1 __

Did a parent or other adult in the household often or very often... Push, grab, slap, or throw something at you? or Ever hit you so hard that you had marks or were injured?

   No___If Yes, enter 1 __

Did an adult or person at least 5 years older than you ever... Touch or fondle you or have you touch their body in a sexual way? or Attempt or actually have oral, anal, or vaginal intercourse with you?

   No___If Yes, enter 1 __

SAFE

Did you often or very often feel that ... No one in your family loved you or thought you were important or special? or Your family didn't look out for each other, feel close to each other, or support each other?

No___If Yes, enter 1 ___

Did you often or very often feel that ... You didn't have enough to eat, had to wear dirty clothes, and had no one to protect you? or Your parents were too drunk or high to take care of you or take you to the doctor if you needed it?

No___If Yes, enter 1 ___

Were your parents ever separated or divorced?

No___If Yes, enter 1 ___

Was your mother or stepmother:
Often or very often pushed, grabbed, slapped, or had something thrown at her? or Sometimes, often, or very often kicked, bitten, hit with a fist, or hit with something hard? or Ever repeatedly hit over at least a few minutes or threatened with a gun or knife?

No___If Yes, enter 1 ___

Did you live with anyone who was a problem drinker or alcoholic, or who used street drugs?

No___If Yes, enter 1 ___

SAFE

Was a household member depressed or mentally ill, or did a household member attempt suicide?

No___If Yes, enter 1 __

Did a household member go to prison?

No___If Yes, enter 1 __

Now add up your "Yes" answers: _____ This is your ACE Score.

References

ACEs Science 101. (n.d.). Retrieved from ACEs Too High : https://acestoohigh.com/

Allen, J. P., Pianta, R. C., Gregory, A., Mikami, A. Y., & Lun, J. (2011). An Interaction-Based Approach to Enhancing Secondary School Instruction and Student Achievement. *Science*, 1034-1037.

Clute, S. (n.d.). *Unitive Education.* Retrieved from The Alliance for Unitive Justice: www.a4uj.org/unitive-education-school-programs

Deci. Edward, L., & Ryan, R. M. (2000). The "What" and "Why" of Goal Pursuits; Human Needs and the Self-Determination of Behavior. *Psychological Inquiry, 11*(4), 227.

Desmond, M. (2016). *Evicted: Poverty and Profit in the American City.* New York: Penguin Random House.

Doepke, M., & Zilibotti, F. (2019). *Love, Money and Parenting: How Economics Explains the Way We Raise Our Kids.* Princeton: Princeton University Press.

Gregory, A., Hafen, C. C., Ruzek, E., Mikami, A. Y., Allen, J. P., & Pianta, R. C. (2016). Closing the Racial Discipline Gap in Classrooms by Changing Teacher Practice. *School Psychology Review*, 171-191.

Kohn, A. (1993). *Punished by Rewards.* New York: Houghton Mifflin Company.

LeDoux, J. (2015). *Anxious: Using the Brain to Understand and Treat Fear and Anxiety.* New York: Penguin Random House .

Lieberman, M. D. (2014). *Social: Why Our Brains Are Wired to Connect.* New York: Broadway Books.

Markovits, D. (2019). *The Meritocracy Trap: How America's Foundational Myth Feeds Inequality, Dismantles the Middle Class, and Devours the Elite.* New York: Penguin Press.

Mullainathan, S., & Shafir, E. (2013). *Scarcity: Why Having So Little Means So Much.* New York: Henry Holt and Company.

National Scientific Council on he Developing Child. (2010). *Early Experiences Can Alter Gene Expression and Affect Long-Term Development: Working Paper No. 10.* Retrieved from Center on the Developing Child Harvard University: www.developingchild.harvard.edu

National Scientific Council on the Developing Child. (2010). *Persistent Fear and Anxiety Can Affect Young Children's Learning and Development: Working Paper No.9.* Retrieved from Center on the Developing Child Harvard University: www.developingchild.harvard.edu

National Scientific Council on the Developing Child. (2011). *Building the Brain's "Air Traffic Control" System: How Early Experiences Shape the Development of Executive Function: Working Paper #11.* Retrieved from Center on the Developing Child: Harvard University: www.developingchild.harvard.edu

Pianta, R. C. (2011, November). *Teaching Children Well: New Evidence-Based Approaches to Teacher Professional*

Development and Training. Retrieved from Center for
American Progress: www.americanprogress.org

Porges, S. W. (2004, May). Neuroception: A Subconscious
System for Detecting Threats and Safety. *Zero to Three,*
19-24.

Porges, S. W. (2011). *The Polyvagal Theory: Neurophysiological
Foundations of Emotions, Attachment, Communication,
Self-Regulation .* New York: W. W. Norton and
Company.

Santoro, D. A., & Berliner, D. C. (2018). *Demoralized: Why
Teachers Leave the Profession They Love and How They
Can Stay.* Cambridge, Ma: Harvard Education Press.

Sapolsky, R. M. (1994). *Why Zebra's Don't Get Ulcers.* New York:
Henry Holt and Company.

Schweinhart, L. J., & Weikart, D. P. (1997). The High/Scope
Preschool Curriculum Comparison Study Through Age
23. *Early Childhood Research Quarterly,* 117-143.

Sege, R. D., Siegel, B. S., & Council on Child Abuse and Neglect,
C. o. (2018, December). *Policy Statement: Effective
Discipline to Raise Healthy Children.* Retrieved from
American Academy of Pediatrics:
https://pediatrics.aappublications.org/content/142/6/e
20183112

Seligman, M. E. (2006). *Learned Optimism.* New York: Random
House.

Siegel, D. J. (2013). *Brainstorm: The Power and Purpose of the
Teenage Brain.* New York: Jeremy P. Tarcher/Penguin.

Souers, K., & Hall, P. (2016). *Fostering Resilient Learners: Strategies for Creating a Trauma-Sensitive Classroom.* Alexandria, Va: ASCD.

Starseed, S. P. (2011). *The Ecology of Learning: Re-Inventing Schools.* Richmond, Va: Amazon.

Starseed, S. P. (2012, Spring). The Fallout from Fight-or-Flight. *S.I. Focus Magazine*, pp. 12-15.

Van Der Kolk, B. (2014). *The Body Keeps the Score: Brain, Mind, and Body in the Healing of Trauma.* New York: Penguin Random House.

Wilkinson, R., & Pickett, K. (2009). *The Spirit Level: Why Greater Equality Makes Societies Stronger.* New York: Bloomsbury Press.

Wilkinson, R., & Pickett, K. (2019). *The Inner Level: How More Equal Societies Reduce Stress, Restore Sanity and Improve Everyone's Well-being.* United Kingdom: Penguin Books.

ACKNOWLEDGEMENTS

I am deeply grateful to everyone who has helped me on the journey of this book. Thanks to Avis Binford, Terrie Buczek, Linda Childs, Pamela Donison, Gail Poulton, Chris Verner, and Janet Williams for their insightful feedback on the manuscript. I am especially grateful to Robert Bushman for his editorial assistance throughout and his editing of the final copy. Special thanks to Talia Moser for her generosity, skill, and patience in producing the cover for SAFE. Thank you all!

ABOUT THE AUTHOR

Suzanne P. Starseed is author of *The Ecology of Learning: Re-Inventing Schools*. She has contributed to video scripts for public broadcasting and numerous organizations that promote a more peaceful, just, and sustainable world.

Made in the USA
Columbia, SC
10 February 2021